THE PUNCH BOOK OF GOLF

THE PUNCH BOOK
OF
GOLF

Compiled by
Susan Jeffreys

Foreword by
Peter Alliss

A PUNCH BOOK

Published in association with

GRAFTON BOOKS

A Division of the Collins Publishing Group

Grafton Books
A Division of the Collins Publishing Group
8 Grafton Street, London W1X 3LA

Published by Grafton Books 1986

British Library Cataloguing in Publication Data

The Punch book of golf.
1. Golf – Anecdotes, facetiae, satire, etc.
I. Jeffreys, Susan
827'.914'080355   GV967

ISBN 0-246-13057-1

Printed in Great Britain by
William Collins Sons & Co. Ltd,
Westerhill, Glasgow

Contents

List of Contributors		vii
Foreword *by Peter Alliss*		ix
1	Rules of the Game	1
2	Club and Clubhouse	8
3	Courses and Fairways	25
4	Play and Players	45
5	Women on the Links	65
6	Kit	90
7	Ploys and Gambits	101
8	Caddies	121
9	Champions and Championships	137
10	Indoor Golf	167

List of Contributors

Writers

Bertram Atkey 25
John Betjeman 33
C. L. M. Brown 90
Mr Clarke 65
Alfred Cochrane 141
Alan Coren 95
Peter Dickinson 50
P. B. Durnford 70
Charles Geake 65
C. L. Graves 27, 138
L. B. Gullick 47, 101
A. P. Herbert 1
Susan Jeffreys 175
Frank Keating 157, 160, 164
Miles Kington 6, 117
E. V. Knox 107, 142, 144
Henry Longhurst 37
Fergusson Maclay 147
George C. Nash 11, 31, 93
F. G. Penney 74
Gordon Phillips 47
Chris Plumridge 126
Stephen Potter 110
R. H. Risk 45
Stanley Salvidge 137
Turley Smith 68
J. R. Stagg 121
David Taylor 156
E. S. Turner 4
Eric Walmsley 113
Keith Waterhouse 21
Ralph Wotherspoon 8, 49, 124

Cartoonists

Atchison 115
H. M. Bateman 10, 78
A. E. Beard 149
Beauchamp 133
Brockbank 32, 137, 170
Hector Breeze 173
Eric Burgin 112, 170
Cavalier 38
Claude 55
Cookson 174
G. S. Dixon 72
Du Maurier 138
Emett 94, 95
ffolkes 5, 39, 100, 134
Fitz 30, 139
Noel Ford 179, 180
Ghilchick 80
Graham 14, 16, 40, 42, 54–6, 58,
    60, 83–5, 150, 169, 176
Handelsman 60, 61
Tony Husband 22
Ionicus 33, 54, 148, 169
Jensen 160
David Langdon 34, 62, 86, 87,
    116, 152, 154, 158
Larry 61, 98, 175
S. McMurtry 57, 174
Mahood 36, 84, 135
Norman Mansbridge 88
Leslie B. Martin 130
Phil May 44
Minet 173
Nick 43
Bernard Partridge 104
Norman Pett 126

Bertram Prance 53, 74, 82, 91, 130, 131, 132
Peter Probyn 96
L. Raven Hill 50
Rees 57
Frank Reynolds 68, 71, 73, 75–6, 81, 92, 102, 106, 109, 123, 127, 167, 168
Ridgewell 2, 49, 51
Harry Rowntree 125
W. Scully 88, 154
E. H. Shepard 29
Siggs 83
Francis Smilby 114
A. T. Smith 66, 122, 124
G. L. Stampa 129
Starke 13, 37, 53, 85, 89, 137, 171, 172
David Taylor 119
J. W. Taylor 19, 35, 56, 86–7, 100, 117, 118, 135, 143, 151, 155, 178
Thelwell 83, 171, 179
Bert Thomas 26, 48, 128, 134
J. H. Thorpe 24, 52, 77, 108, 140
Bill Tidy 64, 155
F. H. Townsend 69, 72
Trog 156
A. Wallis Mills 9, 46, 67
Arnold Wiles 20
Frank Wilson 110, 111

Foreword

by Peter Alliss

Have you noticed how rare it is to see real humour in print? Verbal stories well told generally have the edge over the written word, as do cartoonists whose skills I envy for their ability to conjure up the funny side of life with a simple drawing and just a few words. It is curious how some sports or pastimes generate a tremendous amount of humour and others hardly any at all. How many jokes have you heard that feature, for instance, bowls, swimming, archery, athletics, tennis, rowing or shotputting?

Rugby, boxing and soccer certainly have their supporters, and the game of cricket generates a vast body of humour, but surely it's the game of golf that brings about the most smiles. Why should that be?

Perhaps it's just because golf is so essentially different to all the others. For example, how many games do you know where the object of the exercise is to score as low as possible? Not many, I vow. The golfing arena is, on average, about 100 acres or so; 35 to 40 of these are carefully prepared green swards ready to receive a white sphere 1.68 inches in diameter whose ultimate destination is a four-and-a-half-inch hole set in the most beautifully prepared grass on the whole estate. Trees, lakes, heather, gorse, ditches and out-of-bounds fences all lie in wait for the unwary, rather like some Royal Marine assault course: a good walk spoilt. But for the vast majority of people golf is a means of exercise, and provides opportunities for social intercourse and for venting one's feelings on that wretched little ball that clearly has no caring feelings for whatever is about to happen to it.

Throughout the years *Punch* has produced a gallery of wonderful golfing characters: Colonel Bogie, the Flapper, the Bully, the Club Bore, the Professional, the Steward, the Head Greenkeeper, the Secretary, the Lady Captain, the President, the New Member, the Caddies, as well as the Club's animals – the dogs, cats, and even that damned parrot the Steward keeps in his quarters; there are also the Bank Managers, the Car and Insurance salesmen and all the other characters you find at most golf clubs throughout the length and breadth of the land. The Junior Section invariably wins all the competitions during the school holidays, much to the chagrin of the older members; and the arguments in committee go on for hours – whether to change the colour of the curtains in the Ladies' Locker Room or to paint the Men's Bar. Oh, what a glorious pageant it all is! And what a feast of enjoyable reading this book's many passages, stories and cartoons from bygone days provide! (Times that, sadly, will never be recaptured.)

For me, golf has not always been an easy passage, but I am exceptionally privileged that it has played such a large part in my life. It has given me everything: a good living, certainly, but above all a sense of fair play and fun, the opportunity to travel and meet people in all four corners of the world, and during those travels to take time off to watch, admire and laugh with – and sometimes shed a tear for – those who have demonstrated courage, folly, honesty, and at times a little dishonesty, all that goes to make up the funny old game of golf.

A toast then to golf. A wonderful, delightfully absurd game that is unique in its structure, for it can be enjoyed alone or with groups large and small. Young or old, boys or girls – long may golf, and its humour, survive and prosper.

CHAPTER ONE

Rules of the Game

Misleading Cases

IS A GOLFER A GENTLEMAN?

Rex v. Haddock

Before the Stipendiary

This case, which raised an interesting point of law upon the meaning of the word 'gentleman', was concluded today.

The Stipendiary, giving judgment, said: 'In this case the defendant, Mr Albert Haddock, is charged, under the Profane Oaths Act, 1745, with swearing and cursing on a Cornish golf-course. The penalty under the Act is a fine of one shilling for every day-labourer, soldier or seaman, two shillings for every other person under the degree of gentleman, and five shillings for every person of or above the degree of gentleman – a remarkable but not, unfortunately, unique example of a statute which lays down one law for the rich and another (more lenient) for the poor. The fine, it is clear, is leviable not upon the string or succession of oaths, but upon each individual malediction (see *Reg.* v. *Scott*, (1863) 33 L.J.M. 15). The curses charged, and admitted, in this case are over four hundred in number, and we are asked by the prosecution to inflict a fine of one hundred pounds, assessed on the highest or gentleman's rate at five shillings a swear. The defendant admits the offences but contends that the fine is excessive and wrongly calculated, on the curious ground that he is not a gentleman when he is playing golf.

'He has reminded us, in an able argument, that the law takes notice, in many cases, of such exceptional circumstances as will break down the normal restraints of a civilised citizen and so powerfully inflame his passions that it would be unjust and idle to apply to his conduct the ordinary standards of the law, as for example where without warning or preparation he discovers another man in the act of molesting his wife or family. The law recognises that under such provocation a reasonable man ceases for the time being to be a reasonable man; and the defendant maintains that in the special circumstances of his offence a gentleman ceases to be a gentleman and should not be judged or punished as such.

'Now what were these circumstances? Broadly speaking, they were the 12th hole on the —— golf-course, with which most of us in this court are familiar. At that hole the player drives (or does not drive) over an inlet of the sea, which is enclosed by cliffs some sixty feet high. The defendant has told us that he never drives over, but always into, this inlet or Chasm, as it is locally named. A moderate if not sensational player on other sections of the course, before this obstacle his normal powers invariably desert him. This, he tells us, has preyed upon his mind; he has registered, it appears, a kind of a vow, and year after year, at Easter and in August, he returns to this county, determined ultimately to overcome the Chasm.

'Meanwhile, unfortunately, his tenacity has become notorious. It is the normal procedure, it appears, if a ball is struck into the Chasm, to strike a second, and, if that should have no better fate, to abandon the hole. The defendant tells us that in the past he has struck no fewer than six or seven balls in this way, some rolling gently over the cliff and some flying far and high out to sea. But recently, grown fatalistic, he has not thought it worth while to make even a second attempt, but has immediately followed his first ball into the Chasm, and there, among the rocks, small stones and shingle, has hacked at his ball with the appropriate instrument until some lucky blow has lofted it on to the turf above, or, in the alternative, until he has broken his instruments or suffered some injury from flying fragments of rock. On one or two occasions a crowd of holiday-makers and local residents has gathered on the cliff and foreshore to watch the defendant's indomitable struggles and to hear the verbal observations which have accompanied them. On the date of the alleged offences a crowd collected of unprecedented dimensions, but so intense was the defendant's concentration that he did not, he tells us, notice their presence. His ball had more nearly traversed the gulf than ever before; it struck the opposing cliff but a few feet from the summit, and nothing but an adverse gale of exceptional ferocity prevented success. The defendant therefore, as he conducted his customary excavations among the boulders of the Chasm, was possessed, he tells us, by a more than customary fury. Oblivious of his surroundings, conscious only of the will to win, for fifteen or twenty minutes he lashed his battered ball against the stubborn cliffs until at last it triumphantly escaped. And before, during, and after every stroke he uttered a number of imprecations of a complex character which were carefully recorded by an assiduous caddie and by one or two of the spectators. The defendant says that he recalls with shame a few of the expressions which he used, that he has never used them before, and that it was a shock to him to hear them issuing from his own lips; and he says quite frankly that no gentleman would use such language.

Novice (to particularly keen opponent). "NOW, CHARLES, PLAY THE GAME. NO BLOWING."

'Now this ingenious defence, whatever may be its legal value, has at least some support in the facts of human experience. I am a golf-player myself – (*Laughter*) – but, apart from that, evidence has been called to show the subversive effect of this exercise upon the ethical and moral systems of the mildest of mankind. Elderly gentlemen, gentle in all respects, kind to animals, beloved by children and fond of music, are found in lonely corners of the Downs hacking at sand-pits or tussocks of grass and muttering in a blind ungovernable fury elaborate maledictions which could not be extracted from them by robbery with violence. Men who would face torture without a word become blasphemous at the short fourteenth. And it is clear that the game of golf may well be included in that category of intolerable provocations which may legally excuse or mitigate behaviour which is not otherwise excusable, and that under that provocation the reasonable or gentle man may reasonably act like a lunatic or lout, and should be judged as such.

'But then I have to ask myself, What does the Act intend by the words "*of or above the degree of gentleman*"? Does it intend a fixed social rank or a general habit of behaviour? In other words, is a gentleman legally always a gentleman, as a duke or a solicitor remains unalterably a duke or a solicitor? For if this is the case the defendant's argument must fail. The prosecution say that the word "degree" is used in the sense of "rank". Mr Haddock argues that it is used in the sense of an university examination, and that, like the examiners, the Legislature divides the human race, for the purposes of swearing, into three vague intellectual or moral categories, of which they give certain rough but not infallible examples. Many a First-Class man has taken a Third, and many a day-labourer, according to Mr Haddock, is of such a high character that under the Act he should rightly be included in the First "degree". There is certainly abundant judicial and literary authority for the view that by "gentleman" we mean a personal quality and not a social status. We have all heard of "Nature's gentlemen". "Clothes do not make the gentleman," said Lord Arrowroot in *Cook* v. *The Mersey Docks and Harbour Board*,

(1897) 2 Q.B., meaning that a true gentleman might be clad in the foul rags of an author. In the old maxim "Manners makyth man" (see *Charles* v. *The Great Western Railway*), there is no doubt that by "man" is meant "gentleman", and that "manners" is contrasted with wealth or station. Mr Thomas, for the prosecution, has quoted against these authorities an observation of the poet SHAKESPEARE that

'"The Prince of Darkness is a gentleman,"

but quotations from SHAKESPEARE are generally meaningless and always unsound. This one, in my judgment, is both. I am more impressed by the saying of another author (whose name I forget) that the King can make a nobleman, but he cannot make a gentleman.

'I am satisfied therefore that the argument of the defendant has substance. Just as the reasonable man who discovers his consort in the embraces of the supplanter becomes for the moment a raving maniac, so the habitually gentle man may become in a bunker a violent unmannerly oaf. In each case the ordinary sanctions of the law are suspended; and, while it is right that a normally gentle person should in normal circumstances suffer a heavier penalty for needless imprecations than a common seaman or cattle-driver, for whom they are part of the tools of his trade, he must not be judged by the standards of the gentle in such special circumstances as provoked the defendant.

'That provocation was so exceptional that I cannot think it was contemplated by the framers of the Act; and had golf at that date been a popular exercise I have no doubt that it would have been dealt with under a special section. I find therefore that this case is not governed by the Act. I find that the defendant at the time was not in law responsible for his actions or his speech, and I am unable to punish him in any way. For his conduct in the Chasm he will be formally convicted of Attempted Suicide while Temporarily Insane, but he leaves the court without a stain upon his character.'

A. P. Herbert
10.8.1927

(*Reproduced by permission of Lady Herbert and Methuen London Ltd*)

Please Replace the Cromlech

The Case Law of Golf

Nobody, I hope, ever suggested that golf was a game. Demonstrably, it is a clash of forensic, even ferrety, cunning in which the prize goes to the man with the soundest knowledge of case law; that is, the man who has taken the trouble to digest the *Decisions on the Rules by the Rules of Golf Committees of the Royal and Ancient Golf Club of St Andrews and the US Golf Association upon queries submitted to them by golf clubs, golf associations and golf unions* published by the indispensable *Golfer's Handbook* (or Club-House Lawyer's *Vade Mecum*).

Here one may read the rulings in such history-making cases as these:

The player who removed the top stone from a drystone wall lest it should interfere with his swing;

The player who laid both palms on a freezing green to melt the ice particles in the path of his putt;

The husband who caddied for his wife in a match contest and kept taking her hands to show her how to play the shots;

The man who nipped off to the club-house during match play to fetch a jacket for his partner;

The ball which fell in a heap of grass cuttings, which were finally adjudged to be ground under repair.

Clearly, this great *corpus* of precedents has taken many years to assemble. The unnamed players who bickered about balls in gorse bushes in this continent or that, who disputed the right to rotate a ball in black mud in order to identify it, who laid unauthorised hands on flagsticks, who walked in seething enmity to the club-house because A had asked B's caddy, 'What's the distance?' may long since have passed on to a happier fairway, but humanity – or at all events, golf – is the richer for their legacy.

Generations unborn will profit by the story of B, who was told by a caddie at the second hole that A was carrying 15 clubs instead of 14, but very decently decided to make no protest unless, of course, A won; by ill luck A did win and B thus had no option, as an honest golfer, but to denounce him. The Royal and Ancient endorsed A's disqualification, but put on record their opinion that B's action was 'very unsporting'.

Why they dragged sport into this is hard to see. The soft-minded, who have no place in golf, might think the Royal and Ancient had ruled unsportingly in the case of the player who had just started his swing when the head fell off his club – the sort of thing which could happen to anybody, even the president of the Royal and Ancient. The player evidently thought he was entitled to another attempt with a stouter club, but the law-givers ruled that, even though he did not hit the ball, the stroke counted – 'the intention to strike at and move the ball is admitted.' Another petitioner befuddled by ideas of sportsmanship thought that his opponent (who won) should have been penalised for throwing down his club in a tizzy after failing to shift his ball from a bunker, but the ruling was that unless the player's tantrums were such as to assist the subsequent extrication of the ball (as by flattening the terrain) his grounding of the club was not to be penalised.

Many of the disputes obviously created great tension at the time. In one case it is admitted that things were said which should not have been said and that a player exclaimed 'If you want the so-and-so hole you can have it!' But the outcome of a disputed round of golf is not something to be decided in a fit of pique or impatience or generosity; it can only be satisfactorily determined, perhaps weeks later, in the court of ultimate appeal at St Andrews.

A good many rulings suggest that a low level of competence and knowledge is prevalent among golfers. Some of them seek permission to chalk their clubs, apparently under the impression that they are playing snooker. Others knock their balls into birds' nests and then stand about arguing whether a bird's nest is an immovable object; and when birds take predictable revenge by carrying off balls in play they debate whether birds are outside agencies. One player was about to sink a ball which hung on the lip of the hole when an outside agency in the form of a bee alighted on it and pushed it in; it is easy to picture how everybody went on and on about that. Other

golfers wander about the rough looking for lost balls and then drop new ones, unaware that they have holed out in one; surely the first place a reasonably proficient golfer would look for his ball is in the hole? Women are just as bad. A woman player fossicking in mud for her ball shook her club and the mud-caked ball fell off it. She was not surprised, or should not have been, when the cry at once went up that this constituted a stroke.

From one club came a complaint that balls were apt to get trapped in a cromlech or ancient Druidical monument and become absolutely unplayable. 'Can we regard the cromlech as an obstruction?' was the query. The law-givers knew better than to rule that a cromlech was a movable impediment, but clearly they were not impressed at the thought of a golfer being unable to blast his way from under a dolmen or two. 'A player must at all times adjust his or her play to the course as it is or suffer the consequences,' they said, frostily.

Yet the same pundits showed inconsistency when considering the case of A who refused to let B move a sheet of newspaper in a bunker. A's feeling, one can readily see, was that litter is a permanent and integral feature of the countryside and should be accepted as such. The Royal and Ancient sided with B, instead of directing him to play the course as he found it. If a man is expected to adjust himself to a cromlech, why cannot he adjust himself to a loose sheet of the *Sunday Mirror*?

The Royal and Ancient do not welcome any attempt by lower tribunals to temper the severity of their rulings. They also chide those petitioners who use words like 'rough' and 'fairway' which are not to be found in the Rules. When the Rules fail to cover some eventuality, decisions are based on equity, meaning the collective whim of a quorum of senior golf statesmen brooding in their fastness over the North Sea.

At this moment the Royal and Ancient in-tray is probably full of problems like these: 'A's ball is trapped under a 1948 Singer saloon, which has been abandoned minus its two off-side wheels on the eleventh green. B claims that this is a movable obstruction, but B is twice as strong as A. They have been there since the Friday before last. Please advise'; and 'Kindly rule on the following: A slices his ball on to a heap of radio-active waste not scheduled as an obstruction and demands that, before playing the shot, his partner should be allowed to fetch protective clothing from the club-house; while this is being contested by B, on the grounds that it will delay the game, a crow removes the ball and drops it beside the thirteenth hole, where it is subsequently nudged in by a dormouse.'

The latest dispatches say that night golf on floodlit courses is the new rage in America. This is going to bring many new headaches. Is A entitled to use a hand torch to find his ball in a gorse bush? Should B be penalised for flashing the headlights of his trolley instead of shouting 'Fore'? Are courting couples, when stationary, to be regarded as loose impediments or immovable obstructions? Come to think of it, it's very peculiar that the Royal and Ancient have not been called upon to consider that one already.

E. S. Turner
15.7.1964

The Rules of Golf:
Family Edition

Rule 1   **The Player**
Any member of a family who seeks to promote the ancient game of golf and does his best to improve its image by spending most of the weekend at the golf course, drinking too much in the bar, spending too much on equipment and losing his temper when his attention is drawn to this state of affairs, shall be deemed a player.

Rule 2   **The Opponent**
Any member of a family who thinks the player would improve the image of golf by staying home to help in the garden, stop the roof falling off, talk to his nearest and dearest

occasionally, and be there when he is needed, shall be deemed the opponent. Her children shall be on her side.

Rule 3   **The Lie**
  i. The Awkward Lie
     If the player shall say that he is slipping into the office to do several hours extra work over the weekend when it is obvious even to a garden gnome with low IQ that no-one takes spiked shoes and gaily coloured umbrellas to the office, nor indeed golf clubs, he shall be said to have been caught in an 'awkward lie'.
 ii. The Improved Lie
     A player may improve an awkward lie *if* he gets signed or personal testimony from his employer and two fellow-employees that he really is going to the office to do some extra work over the weekend. He and his three colleagues may then go off and play golf.

Rule 4   **Suspension of Play for Cleaning, Ground under Repair, Casual Water, etc**
A player may be invited by the opponent to forgo eighteen holes in order to do something about the washing up, the ruinous state of the garden, the large pool which forms under the washing machine every morning, etc. If he refuses this invitation and drives off, he shall be subject to a penalty to be fixed by the opponent.

Rule 5   **Driving Off**
If a player jumps into the car in the middle of the opponent's attempt to keep him behind under Rule 4 and revs away rudely and crossly, he shall be said to be driving off. This is subject to a penalty but not till later.

Rule 6   **Lifting and Dropping**
The opponent may demand that the player give her a lift to the shops or drop her off at mother's, but only if:–
  i. He is not more than ten minutes late for the game
 ii. They are on talking terms
iii. They are not on talking terms
 iv. He has borrowed her car

Rule 7   Hazards

A hazard is any natural obstacle to a game of golf, such as repapering the dining-room, arrival of foreign friends, vicars, cat being run over, sudden death of playing partner, redundancy or collapse of British economy. At the first sign of a hazard a player is entitled to drive off *providing* he promises to be home in time for lunch.

Rule 8   Completed Round

A round shall be deemed complete *if*:–
  i. Everyone in the party has paid for a set of drinks
  ii. Someone has said: 'Time for another quick one, George?'
  iii. George has replied: 'It will not hurt me if I do'
  iv. Someone else has said: 'My God, can that be the time?'
  v. George has said: 'I am sure they will start lunch without me'
  vi. Barman has said to George: 'It is your wife on the phone, sir.'

Rule 9   An Unplayable Ball

A ball shall be considered unplayable if it is:–
  i. Lent to the dog by the opponent's children
  ii. Undergoing scientific experiments by the opponent's children
  iii. Left outdoors for more than six months by the opponent's children

Rule 10   A Lost Ball

A ball shall be considered lost if it disappears:–
  i. Behind the piano
  ii. Over the neighbour's fence
  iii. Into the compost heap
  iv. Into the opponent's children's room

Rule 11   Ball Interfering with Play

If the player is invited to a big ball the night before an important match he may refuse the invitation without penalty.

Rule 12   Maximum of Fourteen Clubs

A player may not belong to more than fourteen clubs, with the proviso that if one club should become unplayable during the season through crowding or rocketing fees he may substitute another.

Rule 13   When the Opponent is Struck

If, after all reasonable effort, it is impossible to convince the opponent of the necessity to play golf, it may sometimes happen that the opponent is struck. If this should lead to the opponent resigning, the player may substitute a new opponent.

Miles Kington
23.7.1975

CHAPTER TWO

Club and Clubhouse

The Essentials of Golf

'Do you know anything about golf?' I asked Pottlebury by way of making conversation with a comparative stranger, and immediately afterwards knew I had made a mistake. I should have inquired, 'Do you golf?' or 'Are you a golfer?' and no evasion would have been possible.

'I should think I do,' he replied. 'I suppose there's hardly a course between here and Strathpeffer that I haven't visited. English and Scottish, I know them all.'

'And which is your favourite course?'

'That is a difficult question,' he remarked judicially. 'Only last night I was arguing about the comparative merits of Westward Ho! and St Andrews. Both are easily accessible from the railway, but if you take your car the latter is to be preferred. You get your life bumped out of you on those North Devon roads.'

'I wasn't thinking of the travelling facilities,' I observed coldly.

'No, of course. It's what you find at the other end that counts. Well then, travelling aside, there is much to be said for Sandwich. The members' quarters are comfortable – very comfortable.'

I must have made a disparaging gesture, for he immediately continued:–

'But, if it's only lunch you want, I advise those Lancashire clubs round Southport. They know how to lunch in those parts – Tweed salmon, Welsh mutton and Whitstable oysters.'

'No doubt your judgment is correct,' I replied, 'but I –'

'And at one of them they keep a real French *chef* who knows his business. I wouldn't wish for a better cuisine anywhere.'

'There are other things,' I remarked loftily, 'besides those you mention.'

'Exactly; that's why I like to see a good bridge-room attached and enough tables to accommodate all comers. They have that at Spotworth. You can often get a game of poker as well.'

'But don't you see,' I exclaimed, 'that all these things are mere accessories and circumstances?'

'That is true,' he murmured; 'they are but frames as it were of the human interest. After all there's nothing to equal a crowd of jolly good fellows in the smoking-room. I've had some excellent times down at Bambury – stayed yarning away to all hours. Some of the best fellows I ever met belonged to that club.'

'You don't talk at all like a golfer,' said I.

Pottlebury laughed. 'I was forgetting. If it's whisky you want you can't beat Dornoch and Islay. We've nothing in England to touch them. Why, I've met some of the keenest golfers of the day at Islay – nothing less than a bottle a day apiece.'

'Sir,' said I severely, 'it is clear that you have never struggled like grim death with an opponent who was three up at the turn until you were all square at the seventeenth, and then found yourself after a straight drive with an easy baffy shot to –'

'One moment,' said Pottlebury; 'what exactly *is* a baffy?'

E. P. White
23.6.1920

Golfing Rhymes

THE SECRETARY

The Secretary seldom is
A man of energy and whizz,
Conspicuous for repartee
And courage in emergency.

Too often he's a hopeless serf,
Replacing breakages and turf,
Striving to suit each member's taste
Lest he himself should be replaced.

Ralph Wotherspoon
16.9.1925

Golfing Rhymes

THE STEWARD

Presiding at the bar,
This man is popular;
He hears a lot
Of tommy-rot,
Like 'Did the eighth in par.'

He never says 'Oh, fie!'
Or 'What a beastly lie!'
He simply grins
And mixes gins
And puts a little by.

Ralph Wotherspoon
23.9.1925

JONES REMEMBERS THAT BEFORE THE WAR THERE WAS A NICE QUIET LITTLE SEASIDE HOTEL, RIGHT
ON THE LINKS, WHERE THERE WERE ALWAYS A FEW KEEN GOLFERS. THIS IS WHAT HE FINDS.

THE TEETOTALLER WHO DID A HOLE IN ONE AND OFFERED CUPS OF
TEA ALL ROUND.

Letters to the Secretary of a Golf Club

From 'Fairplay' (Roughover postmark)
4th January, 1935

DEAR SIR, – I have been told by a little bird that you falsified the Club's last balance-sheet and that you bribed the Auditor not to itemise a large sum of money under 'Secretary's Good-Living Account', demanding that he conceal this under the accommodating entry of 'Sundries'.

It is now quite apparent to a great many members of the Club how you were able to afford your trip to Schnitzwirzel at the beginning of December.

Yours faithfully,
FAIRPLAY

From 'Vérité Sans Peur' (Roughover postmark)
5th January, 1935

SIR, – I accuse you of watering the Club whisky.

Beware the 13th January.

Yours faithfully,
VÉRITÉ SANS PEUR

P.S. – I caught young Pullcork (the page) smoking in the staircase passage on Monday.

P.S. 2. – You have been smelling of liquor lately.

From 'Outraged' (Roughover postmark)
7.1.35

DEAR SIR, – The Ground Staff is going to the devil. I noticed two men leaning on their spades this morning at 11.36.

Your slackness in looking after the Club's interests is becoming more and more proverbial.

Yours, etc.,
OUTRAGED

From 'Nettled' (Roughover postmark)
January 9th, 1935

DEAR SIR, – I have heard it rumoured that you get a rake-off on all cups and trophies supplied to the Club. I can well believe it. Things are coming to a head. Before the month is out you will know a great deal more than you do now.

Yours anonymously,
NETTLED

From 'Casus Conscientiæ' (Roughover postmark)
Wednesday, 9th January, 1935

DEAR SIR, – I beg to inform you that the writer on his own initiative had your horoscope secretly cast late this afternoon.

Kindly note that it shows you to be a doomed man with but one hope for your safety – the very improbable chance that four men will come into your office towards the end of the month wearing snowdrops in their button-holes.

Take warning that it will be to your great advantage to follow their instructions implicitly.

Yours faithfully,
CASUS CONSCIENTIAE

From Ralph Viney, Captain Roughover Golf Club

11.1.35

DEAR WHELK, – I am in receipt of yours enclosing all those anonymous letters and asking for advice and some solution, etc., but, my dear good fellow, you must be half-asleep, for at least seventy-five per cent. of the Club know that they are being written by General Sir Armstrong Forcursue, Commander Harrington Nettle, Lionel Nutmeg and Admiral Sneyring-Stymie with the object of so weakening your powers of resistance that when they make a massed entry into your office on (I think) the 13th January you will hurriedly agree to whatever they ask – in this case your immediate resignation.

Yours sincerely,
RALPH VINEY

P.S. – I take your word for it that there is no truth in the contents of those letters. All the same I have always maintained that there is no smoke without a fire, and under the circumstances I think that you had better put the accusations one by one on the Agenda for the next meeting.

I am sure you will agree that this is only fair to all concerned.

P.S. 2. – If you resign, remember you must give a month's notice.

From Ralph Viney, Captain Roughover Golf Club

15.1.35

DEAR WHELK, – I note from your letter of the 14th that you have patched up a temporary truce with the Big Four, but consider the promise that you would see that their handicaps were all raised by one stroke, provided they left you alone for a month, a very weak one.

If you once start that sort of thing there can be only one end for you – the Bankruptcy Courts.

Yours sincerely,

RALPH VINEY

George C. Nash

23.1.1935

Letters to the Secretary of a Golf Club

From Ralph Viney, Captain Roughover Golf Club, Roughover

10th January, 1935

DEAR WHELK, – In answer to your query, there will be no official opening of the new Hard Tennis Court. Just put up a notice calling both the men and lady members' attention to the fact that it will be ready for play on the 15th January, together with charges, length of time court may be occupied, etc., etc.

We have taken such pains to keep the matter hushed up from the 'Golf Only' squad that it would only irritate them to make a song about it now. In any case I expect there will be trouble enough as it is.

Let me know how the receipts go. I sincerely hope that the court will be a money-maker and give our revenue a much-needed leg-up.

The ladies, I am sure, will be delighted.

Yours sincerely,

RALPH VINEY

From General Sir Armstrong Forcursue, K.B.E., C.S.I., The Cedars, Roughover

Monday, 14th January, 1935

SIR, – I am not in the habit of mincing my words, but I feel that I am hardly overstating matters when I now inform you in black and white that you are an unadulterated liar. For what in the name of fortune do you mean, Sir, by telling me a month ago that the earthworks going on outside the Reading Room window were for a new putting-green when you knew perfectly well, as I do now, that they were for one of those footling tennis courts?

And kindly inform me, Sir, if it is true that you are going to allow members of the Ladies' Golf Club as well as men to play on it, for if this is so it is one of the most degrading things the Committee has ever done, and that, as you well know, is saying a lot.

Yours faithfully,

ARMSTRONG FORCURSUE

From Admiral C. Sneyring-Stymie, The Bents, Roughover

14.1.35

DEAR SIR, – The new tennis court is *really* one of the most appalling blunders the Committee has ever made, and so far as I can see it is but a step now to allowing lady members into the bar and the Reading Room and to vote at the annual general meeting. In fact I understand they have already obtained a footing in the Club in that they are now permitted to use the old cellar in the basement as a dressing-room.

Kindly see that this ghastly innovation of turning our select Men's Golf Club into a Mixed Gossip Party is stopped forthwith.

Yours faithfully,

C. SNEYRING-STYMIE

From Lionel Nutmeg, Malayan Civil Service (Retd.), Old Bucks Cottage, Roughover

16th January, 1935

SIR, – I wish to report that a woman was playing tennis this morning on the new hard court without any stockings; and, further, several of the young men were in white shorts.

Kindly note that if this sort of thing occurs again I shall resign from the Club.

Yours faithfully,

LIONEL NUTMEG

P.S. – The giggling, screaming and squealing was intolerable. There was no room in the Club where these vulgar sounds did not penetrate.

From Mrs Gopherly-Smyte, 'The Cottage', Roughover

Thursday, 17th January, 1935

DEAR MR WHELK, – It is disgraceful that you allow the men to watch the tennis-players from the bay-window in the Reading Room.

I was on or about the court for most of yesterday morning and during the whole time there were never fewer than ten male members peering at us. One – Mr Lionel Nutmeg – sat staring with his nose glued to the pane for well over two-and-three-quarter hours.

Now, Mr Whelk, I absolutely insist that a curtain be put up in the men's Reading Room to give the tennis-players a little privacy. In fact if this is not done immediately I shall refuse to give anything towards the prize for the Mixed Flag Competition in June.

Yours truly,
KATHLEEN GOPHERLY-SMYTE

From the undersigned (Roughover postmark)
18.1.35

SIR, – It is with deep indignation that we call your attention to the fact that a tennis-ball was deliberately driven from the new hard court into the Reading Room at 10.47 this morning with the following result:–

(1) A glass of brown sherry overturned. (Glass, 1/-, Sherry, $9\frac{1}{2}d$.)
(2) A waistcoat ruined. (Mr Nutmeg's.)
(3) A pane of glass smashed (3ft. by 2ft.)
(4) General Sir Armstrong Forcursue's blood-pressure forced up from 170 approx. to over 200.

We are, Sir,
Yours faithfully.
LIONEL NUTMEG
C. SNEYRING-STYMIE
HARRINGTON NETTLE
ARMSTRONG FORCURSUE

'. . . and as for my putting . . !'

'So if one were foolish enough, one would insert one's sixpence here,
I suppose.'

From Mrs Gopherly-Smyte, 'The Cottage', Roughover

Saturday, 19th January, 1935

DEAR MR WHELK, – On behalf of the tennis-players I have no option but to inform you that several male members of the Club have made a habit lately of practising approaching, etc., on to the 18th green, with the result that they deliberately pretend to mis-hit their shots on to the tennis court, which is, as you know, not fifty yards distant from the back of the green.

Kindly note that unless this childish practice is discontinued I and several of the younger members of both Men's and Ladies' Clubs will take legal action against certain parties whose names you are very well acquainted with.

Yours truly,

KATHLEEN GOPHERLY-SMYTE

From Ralph Viney, Captain Roughover Golf Club

22nd January, 1935

DEAR WHELK, – I have just received your letter, but it is entirely your own fault that both the tennis-players and the non-tennis-players have turned against you.

Honestly, Whelk, I thought you had more tact at this stage of the proceedings than to go and put up notices –

(1) forbidding practice approach-shots on to the 18th green;

(2) stating that the penalty for any tennis-player breaking a Club window will be five pounds;

(3) making it compulsory that the curtain in the bay-window of the Men's Reading Room be drawn while the new hard court is occupied.

However, my one hope is that your singular

lack of foresight will bring about a rapprochement between the parties concerned and that it will not be long now before they will bury their differences in uniting against yourself as their common enemy.

In answer to your question, I regret to inform you that nothing would induce me to interfere on your behalf. You have brought the matter on yourself and you must just abide by the consequences. After all, you are paid for that sort of thing.

Yours sincerely,
RALPH VINEY

From General Sir Armstrong Forcursue, K.B.E., C.S.I.
22nd January, 1935

SIR, – Kindly note that a deputation of the tennis-playing members of the Club, led by Admiral Sneyring-Stymie and myself, will make a personal call on you at 3.15 on the afternoon of Friday, 25th January.

Yours faithfully,
ARMSTRONG FORCURSUE

P.S. – Please book the tennis court in my name for tomorrow morning at 11.30. I shall be playing with Mrs Gopherly-Smyte against Lady Norah Spoon and Mr Lionel Nutmeg.

George C. Nash
30.1.1935

Letters to the Secretary of a Golf Club

From Admiral Seymour Bynnacles, D.S.O., H.M.S. 'Drongo', c/o G.P.O., London
23.5.35

DEAR SIR, – I wish to convey to you the sincere thanks not only of myself but of all the officers under my command for the kindness of your Committee in electing us honorary members of the Golf Club during the few days the Squadron was in Grey Rocks Bay, Roughover.

May I also extend to you yourself my personal thanks for the manner in which you went so very much out of your way to do everything in your power to give each one of us such a good time?

Wishing the Club every success for the future and congratulations on the present state of the course,

Yours very truly,
SEYMOUR BYNNACLES

From General Sir Armstrong Forcursue, K.B.E., C.S.I., The Cedars, Roughover
23rd May, 1935

SIR, – I was drawn against a Commander Marling-Hytch in the match between the Club and the Navy on Tuesday, while McWhigg (who has only been a member for three years) was selected to play Admiral Bynnacles.

Kindly note that I shall refuse to play in this event next year unless I am drawn against a man of (approximately) my own rank.

Yours faithfully,
ARMSTRONG FORCURSUE

P.S. – The savouries were half-cold again on Friday, Saturday, Monday and Thursday, and the cheese had a most aggressive bouquet on Wednesday.

From Lieut.-Commander James Hawser, H.M. Destroyer 'Hornbill', c/o G.P.O., London
23.5.35

DEAR MR WHELK, – I really find it very difficult indeed to express my thanks for the arrangements you made for entertaining the Squadron's golfers when we were at Roughover.

Anything I say will be quite inadequate, so perhaps it would be as well if I left it at that; but I don't think I ever remember having had such a good time.

Yours sincerely, J. HAWSER

P.S. – If you ever happen to be down Portsmouth way be sure and look me up.

From Mrs Harrington Nettle, Captain Roughover Ladies' Golf Club
Thursday, 23rd May, 1935

DEAR SIR, – It was perfectly beastly of you to take so many encores at the cabaret show the Golf Club put up for the Navy during Tuesday night's dinner and dance. Poor Miss Whinn never got a chance to recite her 'Rattlesnake in the Bungalow'; and, what's more, I consider the conjuring-trick in which you make all those golf-balls come out of your nose quite the most revolting thing I have ever seen.

I am bringing the matter up at the next Ladies' Committee Meeting, after which you may expect to hear from me again.

Yours faithfully,

GERTRUDE NETTLE

From Richard Hammock (Sub-Lieut.), H.M. Destroyer 'Bulbul', c/o G.P.O., London

23.5.35

DEAR SIR, – I hate troubling you, but could you please tell me the name and address of the very charming girl who was at that wonderful dance on Tuesday night? She had very big blue eyes, corn-coloured hair (ripe), and very small ankles. What she was dressed in I honestly can't remember, but I'm sure you must know who I mean.

Thank you most awfully for the gorgeous time you gave us at the Club.

Yours sincerely,

R. HAMMOCK

From Lionel Nutmeg, Malayan Civil Service (Retd.), Old Buck's Cottage, Roughover.

23rd May, 1935

SIR, – Why was I not asked to play for the Club *v.* the Navy the other day? This is the third occasion since 1924 that I have been deliberately overlooked. I suppose it is because I was once a Civil Servant. I insist on your reply by return. In the meantime I am reporting the matter to the Captain.

Yours faithfully,

LIONEL NUTMEG

P.S. – Why did you not turn Forcursue's dog out of the Reading Room on Friday?

P.S. 2. – I played bridge in the Club yesterday. The cards were filthy, as usual.

From Captain A. Cutwater, H.M.S. 'Drongo', c/o G.P.O., London

May 23rd, 1935

DEAR SIR, – Could you please inform the lady who gave me her late uncle's gold sleeve-

'Some damned economy campaign, I suppose.'

links to take out to her brother in Malaya (where I go next month) that I have lost his name and address?

I fear the cuff of my boiled shirt, on which I wrote it down, must have got torn off when we played leapfrog round the Locker Rooms after the ladies had gone.

She was dressed in sequins and had things in her hair.

Many thanks for one of the most exhilarating parties I've ever been at.

Yours faithfully,
ALFRED CUTWATER

P.S. – The brother grows cokernuts and goes by the nickname of 'Porker'.

From Mrs Gopherly-Smyte, The Cottage, Roughover

23rd May, 1935

DEAR MR WHELK, – I understand you never introduced my Pamela to any of the really nice officers at the Club's dance the other night.

Kindly accept our resignations herewith.

Yours faithfully,
KATHLEEN GOPHERLY-SMYTE

Commander Marling-Hytch, H.M.S. 'Drongo', c/o G.P.O., London

23.5.35

DEAR MR SECRETARY, – I wonder if the head of my No. 2 iron has ever turned up? It flew off the shaft into a bed of rushes when I was in trouble at the 6th during my match with General Sir Armstrong Forcursue.

I would gladly put up a small reward to the finder and pay postage when same is forwarded. I meant to mention the loss to you after the game, but somehow or other it slipped my memory.

Thank you so much for your unending kindnesses during my stay at Roughover. We all had a wonderful time.

Yours sincerely,
VINCENT MARLING-HYTCH

P.S. – I hope the General's blood-pressure is down by now.

P.S. 2. – The Old Man (Admiral Bynnacles) has been badgering everyone for the recipe for your 'Blue Niblick' cocktail. Can you let me have it, or is it a Club secret?

From Ralph Viney, Captain Roughover Golf Club. (At the Hotel Grandiflora, London, W.1)

27th May, 1935

DEAR WHELK, – I hear from several very reliable sources in Roughover that the way you mismanaged the Navy's visit was absolutely disgraceful, and the general impression is that our visitors won't think much of us.

Please therefore put 'Secretary's Incompetence Regarding Entertainment of Guests' on the agenda for the next monthly Committee Meeting.

I shall be back on Thursday.

Yours faithfully,

R. VINEY

George C. Nash
5.6.1935

Letters to the Secretary of a Golf Club

From Ignatius Thudd, Member of Roughover Golf Club

22.11.35

DEAR SIR, – I am getting very tired of the Club catering. On the menu yesterday you had 'Chops, steaks, etc., ready $\frac{1}{4}$ of an hour,' and I had to wait for over eighteen minutes before I was served with my Chateaubriand.

It is high time you woke up to the fact that you are the Secretary of a Golf Club.

Yours faithfully,
I. THUDD

From General Sir Armstrong Forcursue, K.B.E., C.S.I., Captain Roughover Golf Club

23rd November, 1935

DEAR WHELK, – Why can you not keep the cruets, etc., in order? The heads of the pepper-pots are continually stuffed up, and I have caught several people recently trying to clear the holes with their forks. Not only *that*, but I hear on very good authority that the new member actually *blew* one clear the other day.

A further point: Last Friday I deliberately

buried a golf-tee in the big silver mustard-pot to prove your general incompetence, and, as I fully expected, it was still there yesterday.

Kindly make it one of your daily duties to inspect the mustard-pots.

Yours faithfully,
ARMSTRONG FORCURSUE

P.S. – To-day Nutmeg was eating some of that appalling new cheese he persuaded you to get for him. It has a most aggressive bouquet; but it may of course have been N. himself.

From Admiral Charles Sneyring-Stymie, C.B., The Bents, Roughover
23rd November, 1935

DEAR SIR, – There is a Club by-law to the effect that writing materials, etc., are not allowed to be used on the dining-room tables. Commander Harrington Nettle has a disgusting habit of continually counting up his morning score by writing with a fork on the table-cloth at lunch.

He should be reported to the Committee.

Yours faithfully,
CHARLES SNEYRING-STYMIE

P.S. – Nutmeg wrote his name all over one of the menus yesterday and also drew a picture of a Malayan tapir on the back. The Club is going from bad to worse.

From Barnabas Hackett, Roughover
23rd November, 1935

DEAR SIR, – I regret having to call your attention to the following dining-room rule:–

'Provisions other than those served by the Club may not be introduced or used, excepting game and fruit from the Member's own estate or garden.'

I have therefore no option but to report Mr Thudd for not only introducing but also using a pineapple on the 4th, 7th and 12th of this month. Might I also bring to your notice his method of eating this fruit? The Committee should insist on his using a knife and fork, or at all events the latter.

Please also report him for making pellets of his bread while waiting for his steak on the 21st inst.

Yours faithfully,
B. HACKETT

From Ezekiel Higgs, Member of Roughover Golf Club
23.11.35

DEAR SIR, – I do not like the new waitress in the dining-room. She puts me off my food. I suppose you selected her from the other applicants because she uses lipstick and you thought thereby you'd give the Club a little tone.

Sneyring-Stymie tells me she dyes her hair.

Yours faithfully,
EZEKIEL HIGGS

From Angus McWhigg, Glenfarg, Roughover
24th November, 1935

DEAR SIR, – I had the misfortune to have lunch at the Club yesterday, for which I was charged 3/-. I have since been down to the shops in the town and I find that the soup could not have cost you more than $1\frac{1}{4}d$, the fish 4*d.*, the meat and vegetables 8*d.*, the sweet 2*d.* and coffee, etc., $\frac{3}{4}d$.

This amounts to 1*s.* 4*d.*, in which sum I have allowed for coal, service, rates, etc.

When the Club catering always shows a loss in the annual balance-sheet, it is quite clear to me into whose pocket the difference between the 1/4 and my 3/- goes.

Have you ever heard of the 'Prevention of Corruption Act, 1906'? It would be as well for you to read it through very carefully.

Yours faithfully,
A. MCWHIGG

From Commander Harrington Nettle, C.M.G., D.S.O., Flagstaff Villa, Roughover
25.11.35

SIR, – I was given a kitchen fork for lunch yesterday. Also why is it that whenever I have a meal at the Club I always seem to get the dented soup-spoon which General Forcursue threw at the wasp last June? It should be withdrawn from service immediately. It is high time the Club bought a new set of cutlery.

Yours faithfully,
HARRINGTON NETTLE

P.S. – Can nothing be done to prevent Nutmeg from drinking claret with chocolate soufflé?

'*No one* *should move, talk or stand close to or directly behind a player when he is making a stroke, dammit!*'

From Lionel Nutmeg, Malayan Civil Service (Retd.), Old Bucks Cottage, Roughover
25*th November,* 1935

DEAR SIR, – The coffee at the Club is a disgrace and tastes of MUD. In Malaya my Chinese cook always boiled my coffee in a sock, and I always rated it as the best East of Suez. An ex-Resident of Brunei once complimented me on its excellent flavour.

The socks should be well boiled before use.
Yours faithfully,
LIONEL NUTMEG

From Ralph Viney, ex-Captain Roughover Golf Club

25.11.35

DEAR SIR, – I notice that whenever you have a meal at the Club you are always served first and always get the best and biggest helpings of everything.

When you are allowed the free run of your teeth at members' expense I should have thought you had more manners than to allow this state of affairs to continue.
Yours faithfully,
RALPH VINEY

P.S. – I had lunch at Trudgett Magna Golf Club the other day, and they gave me better food than we have at Roughover and at two-thirds the price.

From General Sir Armstrong Forcursue, K.B.E., C.S.I., Captain Roughover Golf Club

27*th November,* 1935

DEAR WHELK, – I hear that Ralph Viney is going about saying that the food, etc., is far better at Trudgett Magna Golf Club than anything he ever gets at Roughover. I have rarely heard anything so mean-spirited and degrading as his running his own Club down like this.

I have just been talking to Sneyring-Stymie, Higgs, Thudd, McWhigg, Hackett, Harrington Nettle and Nutmeg, and they all agree with me that the catering, etc., at Roughover is better than one can get at any other golf club in the vicinity.

I have therefore written to Viney and told him that unless he makes a written apology to you by return he will have a hard row to hoe in the matter of getting matches amongst his fellow-members for the next six weeks.

My ultimatum will be equivalent to his being sent to Coventry.

Yours sincerely,

ARMSTRONG FORCURSUE

P.S. – The Bombay Duck has been getting very tired the last day or two. See that you get a fresh supply before tomorrow.

From Ralph Viney, ex-Captain, Roughover Golf Club

29.11.35

DEAR WHELK, – I am sorry I said what I did about the food at Trudgett Magna being better than at Roughover. As a matter of fact it was all rather a joke, and I only really did it to try to keep you up to the mark.

Yours sincerely,

R. VINEY

P.S. – The salt was all in lumps again today.

George C. Nash
1.1.1936

'The best we can offer you is associate membership of our waiting list.'

The Rough, the Green and the Ugly

A new golfing story by P. G. 'Keith' Waterhouse

A shower of five-pound notes, in all essentials not unlike senior snowflakes, fluttered through the clubhouse window on a light breeze and woke the Oldest Member from the doze into which he had fallen.

'I perceive,' observed a Scotch-and-soda who had strolled in from one of the Mulliner stories, 'that it is raining fivers.'

The Sage motioned him to a chair.

'If I have warned Angus McAngus to zip up the ball compartment of his golf bag once, I have warned him a hundred times. Yet he continues to scatter five-pound notes as if they were rose-petals strewn in the path of Min, the fertility god.'

The Scotch-and-soda looked baffled.

'The connection eludes me. Am I to understand that Angus McAngus carries five-pound notes in the ball compartment of his golf bag?'

'Not invariably,' conceded the Oldest Member. 'On some occasions he may add the spice of variety to the procedure by carrying tenners. On others, notes of an even larger denomination. It depends whom he wishes to bribe.'

'Bribe? Did you say bribe?'

The Oldest Member, retrieving a neglected five-pound note from the waste paper basket with the sharp-sightedness of a well-trained pig which has detected a truffle in the undergrowth, agreed that he had said bribe.

'I need not add that Angus McAngus has become a hissing and a byword wherever property speculators with a handicap of less than four assemble. Our members frown on sordid cash transactions. They prefer to grease the palms of the planning committee either with post-dated cheques or with the offer of an assisted passage to the Bahamas. This is, after all is said and done, a club for gentlemen.'

'Planning committee? Is that the same as the Cups, Trophies and Tournaments committee?'

'It is not, but it may as well be,' replied the Sage, shaking his head gravely. 'Most of our little tournaments nowadays are played between council planning officials and property dealers or owners of large tracts of land. It has even been mooted that Rule 7(b) should be altered so that the President's Cup shall in future be awarded to the first member to land a building contract under par.'

The Scotch-and-soda clicked his tongue in fair imitation of a hen reproving her chicks for not eating up their chopped worm.

'I remember this club,' he said, 'when the only hint of what might be termed hanky-panky was when Alexander Pervington, in order to win the hand of Evangeline Ffitch-Mortimer by causing her rival Gwendoline Prendergast to lose the Ladies' Spring Medal Competition and thus seek solace in the arms of Wilbur Foskitt to whom Evangeline had become engaged in admiration of his brassie shots, was suspected of switching divots on the sixteenth and seventeenth holes. Are you telling me that times have changed?'

The Oldest Member pointed a quavering finger to the far horizon.

'Do you see the block of offices yonder?'

'If you mean the excrescence that dominates the fairway like an enlarged carton of breakfast cereal,' said the Scotch-and-soda with a shudder, 'you may depend upon it that it has not escaped my notice.'

'That edifice,' continued the Oldest Member, 'owes its existence to a foursome consisting of Rollo Pendlebury, the chairman of the district council in our little backwater here; our popular planning officer Lancelot (Tubby) Catherspoon; one Septimus Purvis, of Purvis, Purvis, Purvis and Purvis, the Mayfair development consortium; and a certain Jasper Potts, who is by way of being a building contractor.

'Pendlebury had been practising his backswing and confidence gleamed from his spectacles as he strode, in much the same manner as Tennyson's hard heir strode about the lands and would not yield them for a day, to the first tee. His opening drive –'

'Excuse me,' interjected the Scotch-and-soda in some agitation. 'This isn't a short story by any chance, is it?'

The Sage regarded his listener with the narrow eye of a life president of the Worshipful Company of Plumbers who, upon encountering a youthful slug in the U-bend of

'Apparently, they're friends of your father's, from the golf club.'

a kitchen drain, suspects it of gatecrashing.

'I was merely about to give you a short résumé of the match,' he said coldly. 'If you do not wish for details, suffice it to say that Pendlebury and Catherspoon took the first, third, fourth, fifth, seventh, ninth, twelfth and thirteenth holes, while Purvis and Potts accounted for the second, the sixth, the eighth, the tricky tenth water-hole, the eleventh, and the fourteenth, where they conceded the game.'

'I don't see what this has to do with blocks of flats,' said the Scotch-and-soda sulkily.

'I was coming to that. A cheque for twenty thousand pounds exchanged hands in the clubhouse. I will give you another example,' added the Oldest Member hurriedly as his visitor rose to leave. 'I believe you have just come from the Angler's Rest?'

'Yes. I was driven out by Mulliner, who was about to embark on an interminable yarn about his nephew Brandreth.'

'Then,' continued the Oldest Member, unperturbed, 'you cannot have failed to notice the £15,000,000 Leisure Complex directly across the road from the Angler's Rest bar parlour. Did Mulliner tell you the story of that enterprise?'

'Several times.'

'I doubt that you heard the authentic version. Mulliner, although an excellent fellow in all respects, veers, if he has a fault, towards nepotism. He may have given you the impression that the credit or blame for the Leisure Complex belongs to his nephew Auberon.'

'That is certainly what he volunteered to a small company consisting of myself, a Small Bass, a Gin and Italian Vermouth and a Thoughtful Pint of Bitter,' said the Scotch-and-soda.

'Whereas,' proceeded the Oldest Member, 'the blame or credit for the Leisure Complex may more properly be laid at the door of a quartet of spavined golfers known as the Wrecking Crew. Have I told you about the Wrecking Crew?'

'Yes,' affirmed the Scotch-and-soda with vigour.

'What I may not have told you about the Wrecking Crew was that one of their number was an architect, a second was a chartered surveyor, a third was a town clerk and a fourth was a county councillor who had the ear of a junior minister who, although otherwise blemishless, could no more handle a mashie on the short fifteenth than a six-month-old baby can dance the foxtrot. Came the day of the Visitors' Challenge Cup –'

'I do not wish to interrupt your discourse,' said the Whisky-and-soda firmly, 'but I have an important luncheon engagement and I think you have made your point. You wish to illustrate, do you not, that golf is no longer so much a sport or recreation as an alfresco version of the taint of vice whose strong corruption inhabits our frail blood? Twelfth Night, for your information, III, *ii*.'

'Never mind all that about Twelfth Night, III, *ii*,' retorted the Sage with some asperity. 'If I may make so bold, you have a lot to say for yourself for a Scotch-and-soda who is only supposed to be an extra, walk-on or spear-carrier. Your role, I am sorry to have to remind you, is merely to provide the feed-lines to lead into my story.'

The Scotch-and-soda blanched visibly.

'What story?'

'The story I am about to tell you,' said the Oldest Member smoothly, 'of Cuthbert Dalrymple, Hermione Ironside, the Town Clerk of Salterton-on-Sea, the Borough Architect of the same bracing resort, the chairman and managing director of Seaview Bungalows (Exploitation) Ltd, and a carbuncle on the body politic rejoicing in the alias of Augustus Merryweather.

'This saga of bribery and corruption in high places (continued the Oldest Member, settling back in his chair) begins with a niblick tossed into the twelfth-hole bunker at the Salterton-on-Sea municipal golf-course . . .'

'I am sorry,' said the Scotch-and-soda, 'but I believe I heard the unmistakable sound of a mini-cab waiting to convey me back to the Angler's Rest. Perhaps you will continue this interesting story another time.'

The Sage pinned his reluctant guest's arm with a grip that had warped many a putter in more halcyon, innocent days.

'What,' asked the Oldest Member, 'is it worth?'

Keith Waterhouse
23.7.1975

'*I've been on the waiting-list for full membership for ages, and I see Denis Thatcher's already down for the Winter Foursomes.*'

'EVER PLAYED AT STOKE POGES?'
'NO. MY ONLY OTHER GAME IS CHESS.'

CHAPTER THREE

Courses and Fairways

Golf for Heroes

A huge, grim man in tweeds, with the jaw of a gladiator, sombre, smouldering eyes, and a pair of crutches, who was standing outside the granite-built clubhouse, pointed out the secretary with, I fancied, a boding, rather sinister look.

'You have played so long upon your rather easy local links that you seek a change – something a little more trying, a shade more difficult – and have heard that the Shadow Valley Links have been laid out especially to accommodate those who like their golf made strenuous?' said the secretary, a bland, easy-mannered, enthusiastic gentleman. 'Quite so; you have done well to come here. You must let me show you round the course. I am very proud of it – extremely proud. Yes, I designed it; every detail of the laying-out was completed under my personal supervision. I came to the conclusion that, for really ambitious players, golf generally was too safe, simple, dull – trivial, in fact. But we are not trivial here. One's nerves must be more or less in order if one is to play a good round on the Shadow Valley Links. But you will see for yourself.

'I think we need not waste much time over the first hole; it is comparatively simple. The bunkers seem rather formidable? Oh, one would hardly say that – the wasps' nest inside each of them makes it a tolerably interesting hole, but hardly formidable. I beg your pardon? Oh, yes – wasps, I said. Three nests – one in each bunker. When a ball trickles into the bunker it automatically sets into action – gentle and sustained action – a patent stirrer and poker attached to the nest, so that the wasps are more or less ready to receive the player when he arrives to play out. We use hornets at the fourth hole – it is much more awkward to be bunkered there.

'This is one of the longer holes – a good hole. We call it the Great Surprise. There are no bunkers, you see. It is a clear fairway from tee to flag. Easier than the fourth, you think? Ah, but one has to keep straight because of the pitfalls. The safe fairway is only four yards wide. Either side of that, here and there – dotted about, don't you know – are concealed pitfalls, with lids – trapdoors – covered with real grass, of course. They work on the dead-fall principle, and contain water or tar – five water, six tar. Only two are staked; or possibly three. I really don't remember at the moment. Do you cultivate the pull at all? I should not advocate that shot just here. The hole is a great favourite with heroic golfers. Mr. HENRY LEACH admires it so much that he has written seventeen different articles about it.

'This is the sixth. You see, the green is well guarded. Yes, they are bull-terriers – four of them. Fierce? Oh, so-so – moderately. It is possible to hole out without risk, but one needs to approach very accurately. Hardly a fair test, *I* think, because some men have an inborn dislike for dogs. We meet that, however. We provide long steel rakes, so that a badly played ball can be raked out of the bull-terrier zone. One forfeits the hole in that case, naturally. You see some of the finest approaching in the world at this hole. Oh, yes, they are safely fastened; each dog can only work within the limits of its string – unless the string snaps.

The posts flimsy? Oh, I don't know. Do you think so? We have had no complaints. (Ah, Cerberus, old boy; there you are. Down, sir; the gentleman is not yet a member.) Don't mind him; he's a little petulant today.

'Now, this is really *chic*, the twelfth. The green is under the cliff, as you see. One positively must play a good shot here; a slovenly stroke is sharply punished. Put your ball anywhere but on the green and an avalanche falls upon you. It is loosened by a magnetic-hydraulic device, patented by me. You see the avalanche – up there, straight overhead. Good imitation of snow, is it not? Rather expensive, but one cannot have really heroic golf without paying for it, obviously. We call this the Excelsior Hole. Mr P. A. VAILE considers that the cliff is not sufficiently under-cut to allow the correct amount of over-spin to the avalanche. I begged him to play the hole for himself, but he was of the opinion that it was hardly necessary; he relied upon his calculations, he said. Personally I think he was wrong; we regularly bag our two brace a month at this hole.

'That one with the red flag is mined in every direction – in six places, to be exact. We use the old-fashioned black blasting powder; we find it slightly more effective than gun-cotton. It is fatal to slice there. Mr BERNARD DARWIN thinks it is a very amusing hole. He wrote quite airily about it.

'But you must not imagine that we have neglected the ladies. We are not so ungallant as that, I hope. Indeed, no. Upon the tenth and sixteenth greens are a number of small holes of decidedly menacing appearance. Round about these are sprinkled baited mouse-traps and

Visitor. 'WHAT'S THE COURSE LIKE?'
Caddie. 'WELL, I *DID* 'EAR THAT THEY 'AD TO BURN THE 'OTEL VISITORS' BOOK.'

rat-traps. This is for the moral effect. If a lady makes a bad putt a circuit is completed and an electric current causes a number of mice to pop fiercely in and out of the holes. We have found it very successful. We use snakes also – sparingly, curled up in certain of the holes. The size of the hole, of course, is a draw-back. One rather leans to rattlesnakes; the sudden ringing of their rattles would test the composure of a putter admirably. Unfortunately rattlesnakes run large. A pity; but I am giving some thought to the point, and hope soon to overcome the little difficulty.

'Of course, the idea is really in its infancy. You must not expect too much at first. It is not easy to make golf really heroic, but we shall improve. We welcome suggestions, too. If you have an idea at any time –' he spoke absently, musingly, his eyes fixed rather vacantly on a building close by which looked ominously like a cottage hospital.

'I think you have it all very complete,' I said. 'But there is one thing, perhaps, though probably it is merely an oversight on your part. It would be expensive, I fear.'

His face lighted up. 'And that is?' he enquired.

'An automatic earthquake, or even a pneumatic volcano.'

He beamed.

'Oh, glorious!' he said; 'we will have both. Forgive me, I must telephone to our chief engineer at once. This will delight some of our members.'

He hurried into the clubhouse.

The grim person with the crutches hobbled up.

'How do you like the course?' he asked.

'Oh, very fine, very fine,' I said. 'I am just going to get my clubs.'

It was fearfully annoying to discover that I had left them in London – two hundred miles south – and, as I am not at my best with new or strange clubs, there was nothing for it but to come home for them. It was during the train journey that I strained my back – which, of course, put golf out of the question for a long time.

Bertram Atkey
10.9.1913

How to Save Golf

The controversy which has recently arisen about the overcrowding of championship courses has unfortunately diverted attention from a far more momentous problem. Those who criticise and disparage the game of golf are on strong ground when they declare that it is not a dangerous game. Isolated instances may occur of players who have suffered serious contusions from the impact of a misdirected ball; of players, again, who in the exuberance of their swing have struck other players or even themselves with their clubs. There is the tragic story of an ex-King, who sliced his drive into the tee-box with such violence that it rebounded against his nose, inflicting a wound which confined him to his bed for several days, necessitating the issue of bulletins which appeared in the daily Press. But in the main the casualties of golf are negligible and do not impair its reputation as a pastime conducive to longevity. They do not compare with those involved in the pursuit of polo, Rugby football or even cricket. It is not too much to say that unless the stigma of security can be removed from the Royal and Ancient game it is bound to suffer in prestige and popularity. The charge is beginning to rankle, and only the other day an eminent amateur spoke of it as one of the most serious items in the White Man's burden.

Happily the situation, though grave, is not one that calls for despair or undue despondency. Great evils bring their own remedies, and a glimmer of hope is discernible in the information, published on July 8th, of an incident which occurred on a golf-course in Central Africa. It appears that while a game was in progress a leopard suddenly emerged from the rough and, after mauling a caddy, was beaten off by one of the players. Thus the accusation that golf is not dangerous is shown to be a calumny – in certain countries. Some years ago a friend of the writer, during a visit to India, was playing on a course in the neighbourhood of Calcutta, when to his surprise, while he was putting on a level green, his ball suddenly stopped and began to roll back towards him. For a moment he was inclined to distrust the evidence of his eyes, but his partner, a resident, called out 'Earthquake! Lie down.' My friend obeyed the instruction, and after a few minutes the tremors ceased and the game was resumed.

The importation of earthquakes, though perhaps not beyond the resources of applied science, is hardly to be desired, on the ground that the remedy might be worse than the disease. But the provision of wild animals to enliven the game, to encourage agility in the players and relieve them of the charge of self-protectiveness is a method which is at once more feasible and appeals to the sporting instincts of every true Briton. Hitherto the disappearance from our shores of bears, boars and wolves has confined animal risks on golf-links to the casual incursion of a bull or the rare appearance of the escaped inmate of a travelling menagerie. But these experiences, though exhilarating, have been too few and far between to exert a really stimulating influence on the physical culture of the golfing community. The time has now come for an organised effort to provide them as regular features of the game. And the moment is propitious, because it coincides with the movement to provide sanctuaries for wild animals and to check 'the folly of those' – I quote from the pages of *The Manchester Guardian* – 'who, impelled by sport, commercial interests or sheer ignorance are still bringing wild creatures to the verge of extinction.' The bison, as the same paper reminds us, is not extinct, but it had a narrow escape from becoming so both in Europe and America.

The bison is thus clearly indicated as one of the animals which it is desirable to instal on our links. The claims of the lion, the tiger and the buffalo – regarded by some big-game hunters as the most dangerous of all – are incontestable and need not be discussed. The importation of the larger anthropoid apes raises other questions. It is alleged that baboons have been trained to act as railway porters in South Africa, and there is no reason why they might not be employed as caddies. Elephants again would be invaluable in retrieving lost balls with their trunks. But I think it must be admitted as a governing consideration that those animals should receive preferential treatment which add to the risk of the players and foster intrepidity. The use of any weapons beyond the ordinary clubs or of protective raiment is absolutely to be deprecated.

Lastly, it is obvious that the choice of animals should be dictated by the characteristics of the course. For instance it is not every golf-course where the water-hazards are sufficiently extensive to provide accommodation for crocodiles, alligators or hippopotami. But Sandy Lodge is by its name obviously marked out as a suitable place for the introduction of ostriches, emus and cassowaries.

To sum up, *if golf is to hold its own it must be made more dangerous*, and the Central African incident points out the best way to achieve that end. Incidentally the altered conditions, while possibly leading to higher scores, would completely prevent the recurrence of such deplorable events as disfigured the Open Championship at Prestwick by eliminating from the ranks of the spectators all persons who were not prepared to share the risks of the competitors. The cost of importing and installing wild animals would undoubtedly be considerable. But I am assured on good authority that it would not involve the raising of the annual subscription to the best clubs by more than one hundred guineas for each member.

C. L. Graves
15.7.1925

HINTS FOR MR LANSBURY.

LUNCH-TIME GOLF IN ONE OF LONDON'S QUIETER THOROUGHFARES: COALING OUT AT THE TWELFTH.

DISASTROUS EFFECT OF MIDGET GOLF ON THE LAY-OUT OF OUR LINKS.

Letters to the Secretary of a Golf Club

From Frank Plantain, Greenkeeper, Roughover Golf Club

30th November, 1931

DEAR SIR, – General Forcursue has killed a fine cow while playing the fifteenth hole. It belongs to Farmer Ragwort, who has our grazing rights.

Yours respectfully,   F. PLANTAIN

From General Sir Armstrong D. Forcursue, K.C.B., K.C.M.G., The Cedars, Roughover

30th November, 1931

DEAR SIR, – You will no doubt be interested to learn that I killed a cow stone dead in the rough at the fifteenth hole about 11.57 this morning. My drive, although hooked, carried the hill in front of the tee, and in coming up to the ball I was both astonished and annoyed to find it in an unplayable lie, not a foot from the brute's head.

Should any witness be required, Mr Lionel Nutmeg, M.C.S., will corroborate the above.

Yours faithfully,
ARMSTRONG D. FORCURSUE

From Charles Claw, Taxidermist, Roughover

30th November, 1931

DEAR SIR, – Seeing as how I stuffed the reed-warbler the Reverend Cyril Brassie killed with his cleek-shot on the Links last June, I should like to quote you as follows for the cow General Forcursue dispatched today:

	£	*s.*	*d.*
To one cow mounted in glass case with brass plate suitably inscribed	19	5	0
Wooden stand for same 8 ft. by 5 ft. by 3 ft.	2	8	0 extra

Trusting to be favoured with your esteemed commands,

CHAS. CLAW

From Gwendoline Makepeace, 'Love-in-the-Mist Cottage', Roughover

30th November, 1931

DEAR SIR, – I wish to resign from the Club immediately. It is just too terrible to think that General Forcursue has killed one of the cows; really he has reduced himself to the level of a common murderer, and I am reporting the matter to the R.S.P.C.A. this afternoon.

Yours faithfully,   GWEN MAKEPEACE (*Miss*)

From Marcus Penworthy, Free-lance Journalist, Roughover

30th November, 1931

DEAR MR SECRETARY, – Extraordinarily interesting the General bumping-off the cow, wasn't it? *The Golfer's Handbook* can quote nothing like it; seagulls, weazels and a trout – yes, but a cow – never.

May I write an article about it? I shall give the matter full publicity and will of course mention the Club.

Yours sincerely,   M. PENWORTHY

From Robin Badger, St Anne's Preparatory School for Boys, Roughover
(*Unstamped*)

30th November, 1931

DEAR SIR, – Could you please get the General's signature for me? I enclose my autograph-book herewith.

Yours with best wishes,   ROBIN BADGER

From Alexander Spool, Photographer, Roughover

30th November, 1931

DEAR SIR, – I have taken six photographs of the deceased animal from various angles. Perhaps you could let me know at your earliest convenience the number of finished sets members would require.

Yours obediently,   A. SPOOL

P.S. – *The Roughover Chronicle* are using three positions in tomorrow's issue.

From the County Agent for the Iron Muscle Tonic Co. (1931), Ltd, High Street, Roughover

30th November, 1931

DEAR SIR, – We should be very much obliged if you would approach General Sir Armstrong D. Forcursue, K.C.B., K.C.M.G., with a view to his allowing us to incorporate his name and photograph in our local advertisement. The photo to be in full military dress, if possible. Kindly inform the General that if he is agreeable we would pay him the sum of (7/6) seven shillings and sixpence for each insertion.

We are, Dear Sir,
For the Iron Muscle Tonic Co. (1931), Ltd,

RUPERT MASSAGE

From William Ragwort, The Dairy Farm, Roughover

30*th November*, 1931

DEAR SIR, – My apologies, Sir, for letting that cow Pansy lie on the course today, but I could not get her home yesterday eve. I was up with the beast all night, her having colic powerful bad and with inflammation setting in she died afore daylight come.

I have not labour enough to lift her till to-night, but will do so then.

Yours, Sir,   WILLIAM RAGWORT

George C. Nash
16.12.1931

Wartime Letters to the Secretary of a Golf Club

From Henry V. Neep, County Inspector, Ministry of Agriculture (Temporary Address: The Commercial Hotel, Trudgett Magna)

DEAR SIR, – You are no doubt aware that the provisions of the recent Tillage Order now apply to Golf Courses, and I propose to visit and inspect the Roughover Links at 10 A.M. on Friday, the 13th inst., with a view to determining the amount of your *arable* ground, and coming to a decision as to the best means of utilising the whole area in the interests of increased food production.

Trusting that it will be convenient for you to meet me on this date,

Yours faithfully,
H. V.NEEP

From Lionel Nutmeg, Malayan Civil Service (Retd.), Old Bucks Cottage, Roughover

DEAR WHELK, – I hear an inspector is coming down to see what the Club can do towards the national food effort, and I am writing to tell you that SHEEP are by far the best solution, as this would enable you to preserve the greens and fairways in their present state, save the expense and labour of mowing (owing to the animal's constant cropping activities), and most important of all, bring in an excellent return from mutton and wool.

All you would have to do is to stick the sheep on to the course, hire a herd to keep an eye on them, and await results.

If you cannot find a herd you could easily do the job yourself; it requires no real brains, merely a certain amount of patience.

Hoping you will give this matter your earnest consideration,

Yours sincerely,
LIONEL NUTMEG

P.S. – If you were badly stuck I might be able to give you a hand with the shearing. I once saw it being done in New South Wales when I took three months' leave there in 1911.

Seaside Golf

HOW straight it flew, how long it flew,
   It clear'd the rutty track
And soaring, disappeared from view
   Beyond the bunker's back –
A glorious, sailing, bounding drive
That made me glad I was alive.

And down the fairway, far along
   It glowed a lonely white;
I played an iron sure and strong
   And clipp'd it out of sight,
And spite of grassy banks between
I knew I'd find it on the green.

And so I did. It lay content
   Two paces from the pin,
A steady putt and then it went
   Oh, most securely in.
The very turf rejoiced to see
This quite unprecedented three.

Ah! seaweed smells from sandy caves
   And thyme and mint in whiffs,
In-coming tide, Atlantic waves
   Slapping the sunny cliffs,
Lark-song and sea-sounds in the air
And splendour, splendour everywhere.

High on the grassy cape I stood,
   Calmly addressed the ball,
And with what power I swung the wood
   For the greatest drive of all
And saw it topple off the tee
And tumble down into the sea.

John Betjeman
6.7.1953

From Admiral Charles Sneyring Stymie, C.B.,
R.N. (Retd.), The Bents, Roughover

DEAR WHELK, – I understand that ass Nut-meg has written in suggesting you keep sheep on the course. He is a penny-wise-pound-stupid idiot – surely *even you* have heard that if you plough land that has not been broken up within the past seven years the Government makes a grant of £2 per acre?

The course having some 250 acres under its control, it doesn't require much of a mathematical calculation to discover that the resultant sum would help to reduce the appalling overdraft you deliberately let the Club in for in connection with relaying the 4th and 5th greens, and putting up that ghastly bicycle-shed just because the Rev. Cyril Brassie asked you to.

'Let 'em have it as a rocket base . . . let 'em have it!'

Some fishermen were telling me this morning that a large porpoise (probably a dolphin) has been washed up on the beach. They say it weighs about a ton and was presumably killed by a depth charge. Go down and fetch it immediately; it will only be a matter of time before it makes an excellent stimulant for the new crops.

Yours faithfully,
CHARLES S. STYMIE

From Angus Hare (Artisan Member of the Club),
The Floral Emporium, Main Street,
Roughover

DEAR MR WHELK, – *Re* food production on the links, I proffer the following suggestion, *i.e.*, that all members be responsible for a certain area of ground, *e.g.*, stake them out a claim, say – $\frac{1}{2}$ an acre apiece, and *n.b.* make it compulsory that they till same as an allotment.

Apropos of this I have a nice fresh lot of seeds and artificials just in and would be prepared to make a cut price for large quantities.

I have also just received a consignment of the well-known 'Old Harry Blister Elixir'. It is guaranteed to harden the most delicate hands to the consistency of hide in rather less than nine days. Sample tube enclosed herewith. If you stocked same in the Club House I would be prepared to allow you 1/3 on every dozen tubes sold provided you bought same in one gross lots.

Hoping to hear from you soon,
Yours truly,
A. HARE

From the Honble. Margaret Fitzbutterlegh, The
Combings, Roughover

DEAR MR WHELK, – Don't be a fool, keep goats.

Yours sincerely,
M. F.

From Frank Plantain, Greenkeeper, Roughover
Golf Club

DEAR MR WHELK, SIR, – I was talking to that Colonel Thumb (Club Member) last evening and he was telling me you is to have a livestock farm on the links and I am to be a kind of menagery keeper. Well, Sir the Colonel is a rare man for a joke (my never

having forgot the dead rat he put into Mrs Anderson's golf bag, and it there for months), but Sir, if it is *not* a joke and is a true bill this is to tell you plain and straight I am to leave instanter and go as a fire watcher to the factory in Trudgett Magna, for I was once tramped on by a cow at the age of four years and nine months and have never since got control of my nerves whenever they beasts is about.

It is bad enough having to keep an eye on the rooks, leather jackets, slugs and members without getting more burdens of a similar nature, same all being in addition to the usual routine work and me without a soul to turn to now for hand or help.

The new barrow has fallen to pieces again. As like as not it will be the death of me in due course.

Your obedient servant,
FRANK PLANTAIN

From Miss Gwendoline Makepeace, Love-in-the-Mist Cottage, Roughover

DEAR MR WHELK, – I hear that you may soon be keeping sheep on the course, and so I am taking the liberty of sending you herewith a Balkan shepherd's crook which my Uncle Dick brought back from Bulgaria in 1893.

It has a whistle on the butt for calling lambs and in the shaft a deep two-note horn for scarifying sea eagles and kites (the mouthpiece for the latter has, I fear, been lost).

I felt you simply must have it for the national war effort; every little helps, doesn't it, and I do hope it will be useful.

Won't it be nice when we are able to address you as 'shepherd'? – such a worth-while calling I always think.

Yours sincerely,
GWENNIE MAKEPEACE

From Mrs C. Duff, Daisy Villa, Roughover

MY DEAR MR WHELK, – It may be looking a bit far ahead but I have recently been experimenting on a Wartime Cake Recipe for which the produce you hope to get from the links might eventually come in useful. Here it is:–

GATEAU GOLF DE LA GUERRE

Ingredients

8 oz. Potato flour.
3 tablespoonfuls water.
1 teaspoonful Baking Powder.
6 Saccharine Tablets.
6 oz. bacon fat (obtained by rendering down the rind, etc.).
8 oz. chopped beetroot. (Ref. recent Kitchen Front broadcast and value of same in lieu of candy peel and fruit).

Method

Cream bacon fat and saccharine tablets, add water and beat well. Gradually mix in potato

flour and baking powder. Stir for two minutes before adding beetroot. Turn all into a greased cake tin and bake in a moderate oven for $1\frac{1}{2}$ hours.

At first sight it might appear to be a bit ersatz, but for all that the nutriment value is substantial.

Yours very truly,
CONNIE DUFF

From Henry V. Neep, County Inspector, Ministry of Agriculture, Trudgett Magna

DEAR SIR, – Further to my inspection of the 13th, the Ministry of Agriculture have now instructed me to inform you:–

(1) That all ground West of the stream and North of the County Road be broken up for potatoes. (Points A B C D on the map in your office – approx. 50 acres.)

(2) That the Sea Hollow area be made available for 75 sheep.

(3) That the 12-acre plot known as the 'Old Glebe', East of Club House, be developed as Allotments.

(4) That the 9th, 10th, and 11th fairways and surrounds (*see* map, portion coloured blue) be allocated for the grazing of cattle.

Your immediate attention to this matter is requested.

Kindly note that our Poultry representative will be calling on you on Friday.

Yours faithfully,
H. V. NEEP

From General Sir Armstrong Forcursue, K.B.E., C.S.I., Captain, Roughover Golf Club, The Cedars, Roughover

DEAR WHELK, – Your ridiculous and idiotic letter just received asking what you are to do about the Inspector's letter; but surely the veriest nincompoop would realise without being told that there is only one answer – 'TAKE YOUR COAT OFF IMMEDIATELY AND GO TO IT.'

If Plantain won't look after the livestock you must do this yourself, leaving him to plough with the tractor, etc.

Yours faithfully,
ARMSTRONG FORCURSUE

P.S. – Put my name down for one of the allotments. I will take half an acre and you can get busy hand-digging it for me immediately (double trench).

P.S.2. – I understand several other Club Members, including Sneyring Stymie, Nutmeg and Harrington-Nettle, are going to ask you to do the same.

P.S.3. – This will be a good thing for you as it will keep you warm between the times you are lolling about gazing at the sheep and cattle.

P.S.4. – My wife is also buying $\frac{1}{2}$ doz. goats for you to look after. She says you won't notice them with all the rest of the sheep.

P.S.5. – She has just come in to say they may require milking twice a day, but you can find this out for yourself once you take delivery.

P.S.6. – Since writing the above I have received a wire from my brother-in-law in Glasgow saying that we ought to keep pigs and bees. Kindly see about this.

P.S.7. – I trust you will now appreciate that this is a *total* war.

P.S.8. – *Sic eunt fata hominum.*

George C. Nash
5.2.41

Golf Without Grass

Golf, it has now long since been forgotten, is essentially a simple pastime wherein you start at A and hole out at B, overcoming as best you may such hazards as you encounter on the way, and I am always glad that this is in fact the way I started. My parents had decided to take their holiday in the little Dartmoor town of Yelverton and the year must have been 1921, since I so distinctly remember the man at Glastonbury, where we stopped on the way, with his monotonous chant of '*Old Moore's Almanack* predicts the coming events for 1922.' The hotel at Yelverton overlooked the Common and here two other boys whose parents were staying there had carved out three holes with pen-knives. Soon I had acquired a sawn-off club and together we used to sneak out before breakfast and play two or three rounds. I became completely 'bitten' by

golf and, though I sometimes suspect that I ought to have put such talents as I possess to a better use, the game has been uncommonly good to me ever since.

Both playing it and writing about it began to take me to some of the best, and therefore best kept, courses in various parts of the world, and continuous visits to America ushered me into a world of vast country clubs with swimming pools, masseurs, barbers, and thousand-pound entrance fees. It is excusable, perhaps, if I came to forget about the original simple golf, the sort of golf that was good enough for that great writer, naturalist and fisherman, the first amateur champion, Horace Hutchinson, at Westward Ho!, where, if you found the hole becoming worn at the sides, you took out your pocket-knife and cut another, marking it with a gull's feather for the benefit of those coming behind.

I was brought back to the paths of truth and reality, and have not strayed since, by a visit to the oilfields in the foothills of Persia in the later stages of the war. New faces are always welcome in such parts – some fellows had not had leave for six years – and it was not long before I was ushered up to the Masjid-i-Suleiman golf club, named after the ancient temple nearby. The clubhouse was a fine granite affair, just like home, and the accents of Fife and Glasgow predominated amid the tinkle of ice on a Sunday morning. It was not the clubhouse, therefore, but the course which brought me, literally, down to earth.

Not a blade of grass was to be seen: only a miscellaneous assortment of stones, boulders and slippery mud which bakes rock hard in summer. The greens were of asphalt (the 'pitch' mentioned in the construction of Noah's Ark) and covered by a layer of fine sand, each one of them being attended by a man with a long broom who smoothed out the surface before each player made his putt. As you could not stick a peg tee into the ground, the barefooted caddie boys, some of them quite enchanting little villains, turned up with a lump of clay, out of which they fashioned a tee like a halma man and presented it to you stuck on the bottom of the driver. Sometimes,

as they departed for home, the lump of clay would conceal one of your golf balls. Some of the views were stupendous, and sights and sounds not normally associated with the royal and ancient game enlivened the scene: a man in baggy trousers cantering across the course on a white horse, for instance, or half-a-dozen women walking silently past the green with pots on their heads. *C'est magnifique*, I reflected, *mais ce n'est pas le golf*.

And yet it was. It took only a few holes to bring home to me that here, once more, was the original golf – from A to B, overcoming without complaint the hazard encountered on the way, the complete reverse of the modern conception of playing the same shot with every club in the bag, all 14 of them, and a good shot being assured of a standard result. Here, as in all desert golf, of which I now regard myself as something of an authority, you have to 'manufacture' shots, as indeed you do on the Old Course at St Andrews. To cause a ball to carry an expanse of loose sand and pitch on a firm patch with just the right trajectory to run up through the gully and come to rest on a small circle of fast-running asphalt is true golf. Harry Vardon would have done it supremely well. Jack Nicklaus, I think, would not.

Later I went up to Teheran and here again

'All right. I'll allow you to play the stroke again.'

Dogs on Courses

by GRAHAM

'It's not you he's cross with, silly.'

'Always makes that wheezing noise, does he?'

'She suddenly started to flag at the fourteenth.'

the small European community had made a golf course. Not a blade of grass was to be seen and the course itself was absolutely plumb flat. The greens this time were of a thick variety of grit, or granite chippings, and very tiny, and a ball pitching on them left a dark, bare patch where it landed and stopped dead. Strings of grave, supercilious camels, roped together, would wander across behind the tee or between player and green, their bells clanging mournfully, the drivers huddled up asleep in rugs on the creatures' backs. As we finished our round, maybe a couple of hours later, they were still to be seen, specks on the distant plain, plodding on.

The emigrating Scots have carried golf to the farthest and most unlikely quarters of the globe. A doctor friend of mine, whose practice encompasses several thousand square miles of the Western Arctic, landed to visit some isolated Eskimos. Clambering over rocks and ice on some barren inhospitable island, he looked down and beheld, of all things, a golf ball. The answer, of course, was Scotsmen.

'Sit!'

'We've found his ball . . . now we're looking for his
confounded corgi!'

'We beat him!'

The number of holes had coincided with the number of members: three holes, two Scottish engineers and a Jesuit priest.

Some years ago I visited Das Island, which juts almost imperceptibly out of the middle of the Persian Gulf, little more than a mile long and three-quarters wide – the base incidentally for an operation destined to raise a few hundred millions for the recently deposed Sheik of Abu Dhabi. Never mind the drilling barge, said the accents of Scotland. You must come and see our golf course. There, sure enough, after only three months were nine holes already laid out, the tees built, the greens marked out, and three Indian tailors hard at work embroidering nine flags with the Company's emblem. There was also, by a strange coincidence, Mr Terry-Thomas, the comedian, in whose company I later helped to eat a sheep in Bahrain.

Most of my grassless golf has been played, naturally enough, in the Middle East and many are the comical and poignant memories that return as I look back on it. The course of

'Tenpence? . . . But it used to be only fivepence!'

the Royal Baghdad Club is, or was, in the middle of the racecourse, and last time I was there the overnight rain had turned the alluvial deposit of which it, and indeed most of Iraq, is mainly formed into a kind of reddish glue. There were other excitements, however, since it was a race day. The jockeys ride half way out to the starting post and there dismount for a walk and a smoke while the public lay bets on the totalisator, which, shrewdly enough, they decline to do until they see that their selection is actually alive and on four legs. As we played the short seventh, we had an audience of half a dozen jockeys leaning against the rails, all indistinguishable from Charlie Smirke, as jockeys are all over the world. Their comments seemed to be of a derisory nature but we finished one up, we thought, when the first three of us got on the green and the fourth man hit the stick and nearly holed in one.

Hard by the Eternal Fires through which walked that imperishable trio, Shadrach, Meshach, and Abednego in the days of Nebuchadnezzar and your correspondent in more recent times – they are reduced to a few feet high now but still stink as abominably of rotten eggs – you will find the Kirkuk Golf Club, the course broken up by a few eucalyp-

tus trees and the terrain ideal for golf. A few years ago some bright spirit brought back from Cairo small quantities of a grass which it was hoped might not only survive the climate but also 'creep'. They made a miniature 'green' on each 'brown' and, when I was there, the eighteenth had already 'crept' sixty yards back towards the tee. Perhaps the whole course is covered by now.

It was in Cairo that I had a mortifying experience of grassless golf in reverse. In the Egyptian open championship I was partnered at Gezira with a dignified sheik from a desert course, who played in a nightshirt, from below which a pair of enormous brown boots protruded like skis. He beat me easily. What really hurt, though, was his comment at the end. 'That is the first time, sir, that I have ever played on grass.'

Quite a wide experience of desert golf leaves me with a strong impression that the keenness of golfers varies in indirect ratio with the quality of the course they play on. In other words, the worse the course, the keener they become and the more seriously they take their game. I think of the arid waste of Aden, with the camel sweeping the greens in circles; of Kuwait, which is just one massive expanse of sand, but where you still cannot ground your club in a sand bunker; of Tripoli-super-Mare with the white city dazzling in the distance; and of Royal Benghazi, often inundated by the sea ('but it soaks through and improves the fairways'), where a man told me of the house to which he proposed to retire beside a course in Hampshire and added solemnly, 'I have given my wife a power of attorney that, if the time comes when I can no longer play golf, she is to send for the vet and have me put down.'

Above all, however, I remember El Fasher, in the heart of the Sudan, where they have nine greens, no tees, and one flag, which is brought out each time anyone wishes to play. No good having regular flags since, if they were made of wood, the ants would eat them and, if of metal, they would be instantly melted down by the locals for spears. A boy holds the flag in the first hole till one is near enough for an enormous Sudanese caddie to angle his bare feet behind the hole, whereupon the boy rushes off to hold the flag in the second. One short hole among some particularly repulsive camel thorn, sharp enough to use as gramophone needles, was described by the Governor as 'set in a sylvan setting'. As we neared the end, it was noticed that one of the caddies, wearing a blue diamond-shaped badge on the back of his nightshirt, was getting restive. It turned out that he was on ticket of leave from the local gaol and was anxious about getting back by lock-up. He was thereupon sent back in the Governor's car! I wonder if they miss the British after all.

Henry Longhurst
24.5.1967

'We'll wait here until they've gone, O'Leary.'

Miggs and Griggs, who have got away for a week-end holiday, have strayed on to the Golf Links,
and have been watching the Colonel, who has been bunkered for the last ten minutes –
and the language!!
  Miggs. 'WHAT'S HE DOING?'
    Griggs. 'I DUNNO. THINK HE'S TRYING TO KILL SOMETHING.'

CHAPTER FOUR

Play and Players

The Lost Golfer

[The sharp decline of Ping-pong, whose attractions at its
zenith seduced many golfers from the nobler sport, has left a
marked void in the breasts of these renegades. Some of them
from a natural sense of shame hesitate to return to their first love.
The conclusion of the following lines should be an encouragement to this class of prodigal.]

Just for a celluloid pillule he left us,
   Just for an imbecile batlet and ball,
These were the toys by which Fortune bereft us
   Of JENNINGS, our captain, the pride of us all.
Shopmen with clubs to sell handed him rackets,
   Rackets of sand-paper, rubber and felt,
Said to secure an unplayable service,
   Pestilent screws and the death-dealing welt.
Oft had we played with him, partnered him, sworn by him,
   Copied his pitches, in height and in cut,
Hung on his words as he delved in a bunker,
   Made him our pattern to drive and to putt.
BENEDICK'S with us, the Major is of us,
   SWIPER the county bat's still going strong,
He alone broke from the links and the clubhouse,
   He alone sank in the slough of Ping-Pong.

We have 'come on' – but not his the example;
   Sloe-gin has quickened us – not his the cash;
Holes done in 6 where a 4 would be ample
   Vexed him not, busy perfecting a smash.
Rased was his name as a decadent angel,
   One more mind unhinged by a piffulent game,
One more parlour-hero, the worshipped of school-girls,
   Who once had a princely 'plus 5' to his name.
JENNINGS is gone; yet perhaps he'll come back to us,
   Healed of his hideous lesion of brain,
Back to the links in the daytime; at twilight
   Back to his cosy club-corner again.

Back for the Medal Day, back for our foursomes,
Back from the tables' diminishing throng,
Back from the infantile, ceaseless half-volley,
Back from the lunatic lure of Ping-Pong.

R. H. Risk
2.9.1903

Tiresome Golf Enthusiast. 'THEN OBSERVE THE ABSORBING INTEREST OF THE GAME: THE RHYTHM
OF THE SWING AND FOLLOW THROUGH, THE NICE ADJUSTMENT OF THE APPROACH, THE CAREFUL
CHOICE OF LINE FOR THE PUTT. EACH SHOT A PROBLEM AND SPUR TO THE INTELLECT. SMALL WONDER
THAT GOLF HAS SO GREAT A FOLLOWING. ER – WHAT MADE YOU TAKE IT UP?'
Fed-up Colonel. 'LIVER.'

The Perils of Golf

[According to a newspaper interview 'a prominent physician', when asked whether golf could be regarded as a dangerous game, replied, 'The mental stress is perhaps worse than the physical exertion, especially in the case of elderly people who take the game too seriously.']

By some, I've found,
　It's understood
That golf is bound
　To do them good.
Alas! the book
　Is not so plain –
They overlook
　The mental strain.

They little think,
　As on they press,
The mind may sink
　Beneath the stress:
But, oh, it does!
　At length, perhaps,
With one big buzz
　Their brains collapse.

Golf, I suspect,
　With some I know,
Had this effect
　Long years ago;
Too fiercely racked,
　The works went whizz –
A painful fact,
　But there it is.

Still, do not grieve,
　For, strange to state,
They don't perceive
　Their fearful fate;
As men possessed
　They carry on;
They have not guessed
The mind is gone.

Gordon Phillips
30.5.1923

The Golfing Head

When Grant told me this afternoon that he had given up golf I smiled sardonically and said, 'What, again?' And when he told me the reason I laughed outright. For I have always thought, as no doubt you do, that men do not give up golf except for some terrible reason like floating kidney or paralysis of the diaphragm. And I knew Grant had none of these things.

'My dear chap,' he said, 'have you ever watched a group of pros playing golf? Well, what do you find is the one feature of their swing that is common to them all? A rigid stance? A stiff left arm? A turn of the wrists? A controlled back swing? A sweeping follow-through? No. They do what they like about these things, and they all do them differently. The one and only thing that they all do without fail is to keep their heads down until after the ball is struck.'

'Well,' I said, 'and so?'

'And so,' said Grant, 'I am giving up golf. I have a head that won't stay down after the ball is struck, and, as that is the only thing that matters in golf, it's no use going on playing. That's all.'

This was where I laughed outright.

'But, Grant,' I said, 'you must *make* it stay down. You must exercise proper control.'

'It's no good saying that,' he replied. 'I thought it myself for years; but I know now that it is impossible. There are some heads that won't stay down. It is heredity; it's in the blood. Mine is one of them. And yours, by the way, is another.'

'Thank you,' I remarked coldly and went home.

But, sitting here this evening thinking about my golf I cannot help remembering what Grant said. I have been playing very badly today; I usually do play very badly. Why is it? Is it that I sway my body or get my hands in before the club? Or can it be possible that it is all due to my head? Can it be possible, as Grant suggests, that some of us have heads that won't stay down? It is a fact that I cannot remember one single occasion today when I saw the ball at the moment of impact. Why is it? Why do I look up? Must I always look up? I think of other men's heads – good players' heads, like B.'s and C.'s. Why don't they fly up? Somehow one cannot imagine them flying up. But why?

And then in a flash I remember Grant's word – heredity. Heredity! I picture my father playing a mashie shot; I try to visualise my old grandfather playing a mashie shot. And suddenly I know that it is heredity – that is, in the blood. I see it all. I look at the family crest – with its motto, '*Sic itur ad astra*' – a dexter arm, embossed in fesse, couped at the shoulder in mail, cuffed, or, the hand proper holding a dagger in pale on the point of a dragon's head couped close, dropping blood, gules. Does that sound like looking down? Was it by keeping his head still that the owner of that strong right arm impaled the head of the dragon properly on his dagger? Whose head, I ask you, would have been dripping gules

blood, his or the dragon's, if he had gone about keeping his eye on the place where he had just been hitting? Looking down indeed! Where should we be now, we Tomkinsons, if we had looked down? *Sic itur ad astra!* Am I to be the first of our line to break the glorious tradition? Am I to put the first blot on the escutcheon? Am I to bring up a son who shall say, 'Look at Father, how wonderfully he keeps his head down'? Never. A thousand times never. Not for all the spoons in the Club; not for all the golfing fame in the world. *Sic itur ad astra!*

Grant is right. It is heredity. I think of B. and C. again, with their heads tucked down like the Man with the Muckrake, and I thrill with pride as I pity them for their miserable heritage. Grant is right. I too will give up golf. I will apply myself to some pursuit worthy of one whose head is ever flung proudly up to the stars. I will tell Grant about it at once – tonight.

'WHAT DO YOU MEAN BY PLAYING ON? DIDN'T YOU CALL ME THROUGH?'
'ER – YE-ES, I DID – BUT ONLY IN A HALF-HEARTED WAY.'

First Novice. 'HOW MANY SHOTS HAVE YOU HAD, OLD MAN?'
Second Novice. 'ELEVEN.'
First Novice. 'SO HAVE I. BY JOVE, THIS IS DING-DONG!'

I move to the telephone, my head held high. His wife answers.

'I want to speak to Grant,' I say firmly.

'Hold on,' she replies; 'I'll tell him.' And then she adds with a chuckle, 'He's at the end of the garden, by the garage. He's rigged up a practice-net there, and lit it up with one of the headlights.'

'A what?' I scream.

'A practice-net. You know, he's got some new theory about how to keep the head down.'

'Don't trouble him,' I gasp. 'It's not a bit important.'

And, replacing the receiver, I have staggered into a chair, my head bowed low with sorrow and shame – sorrow for the fickleness of the golfer, and shame for a sudden spasm of envy of Grant and his practice-net by the garage.

L. B. Gullick
31.10.1923

Golfing Rhymes

THE FOURBALL FEARSOME

The Fourball Fearsome habit may
  Be sadly overdone;
I know four howling 'duds' who play
This kind of foursome ev'ry day;
With difficulty and delay
  They drive off one by one.

To minimise the agony
  It might be quite good fun
To get these fellows on the tee
And start all four together; we
Could do it with a 'one, two, three,'
  Or, better, with a gun.

Ralph Wotherspoon
14.10.1925

'IT'S COSTING FAR MAIR TAE MAK' OOR JOHN A GOLFER THAN IT DID TAE PIT HIM THRO' COLLEGE.'

Natural Golfer

From time to time I seem to read about
  The Natural Golfer, some tall peasant who,
    Seeing a scratch four playing, buys a few
Old clubs and plays at once like them. Without
A touch of golfer's ague, or self-doubt,
  His drives scream down the fairway, clean and true.
  When asked about his grip or follow-through
This peasant says 'Ah gives un a gert clout.'

Strangely, such tales are heart-enthralling stuff
  For us, who live some eighty above par,
    Use winter lies from June to June, and play
From ladies' tees, but seldom clear the rough,
  Yet boast about our sixes in the bar.
    We too are natural golfers, in our way.

PETER DICKINSON
25 JUNE 1958

WHY DO WE PLAY GOLF?

SOME PROFESS THEY TAKE IT
UP FOR EXERCISE –

OR BECAUSE OF THE SCENERY –

OR THE FRESH AIR.

OTHERS BECAUSE THEY LIKE
THE OUTFIT –

OR THE SOCIAL SIDE –

OR THE IDEA THAT IT KEEPS
THEM YOUNG.

BUT, THANK GOODNESS, THERE ARE STILL SOME WHO LOVE THE GAME FOR ITS OWN SAKE!

Single Thruster. 'IN THE ORDINARY WAY OF COURSE I SHOULDN'T THINK OF ASKING YOU TO LET ME COME THROUGH; BUT I'VE JUST HEARD MY WIFE HAS MET WITH A SERIOUS ACCIDENT.'

Angry Golfer (held up by inefficient ditto). 'YOU'VE BEEN THERE TRYING TO HIT THAT BALL FOR THE LAST HALF-HOUR. SOME OF YOU PEOPLE SEEM TO THINK YOU CAN DO WHAT YOU LIKE.'

'Fire, sweetheart.'

'I just don't seem to have the time for golf nowadays.'

'*But I understood you were ready*
to talk business, old boy.'

GRAHAM'S GOLF CLUB

'Ah, Constable. Thank God! Back there in the copse by the second tee, woman with a knife in her back – looks in pretty bad shape . . .'

'You need a couple of weeks' work to take your mind off your hobby . . .'

Across The Channel and into the Rough

GRAHAM, who has just returned from a golfing trip to France, marks his card

'Nobody's forgotten their passport, I hope.'

'Hold it, lads! We're in the annexe, four kilometres down the road!'

'. . . and carry two! About 345 yards, a drive and a six iron.'

'If it's a gratte du lapin, or an empreinte d'un sabot de cheval, I can have a free lift.'

'How can we get it across that we only want a quick beer and a sandwich?'

'He's not used to all that wine
at lunchtime.'

'Is there anything in the local rules
about arbres?'

'. . . and who's your French champion, mon ami? . . . . Peter Oosterhuis!'

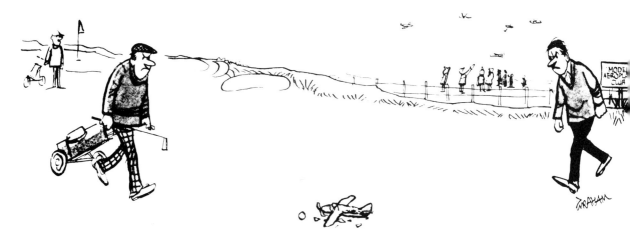

'Whoever you are, this is your lucky day. The
ball hit you just as a doctor and a lawyer
happened to be passing.'

'Do you mind if we play through? We're medical men.
I'm sure you wouldn't want our patients to die because
of some silly delay.'

GOLFING FOR COMMISSARS

DAVID LANGDON

'The Stakhanovite norm for the course is 69.'

'250 yard drive, and that's without steroids.'

'Something in the Ministry of Justice. A comrade of mine beat him 6 and 5 and has never been heard of since.'

'Call me a purist, but the Order of Lenin for a hole-in-one *is* trivialising things a bit.'

'Under R & A Rules, for what I did you simply incur one penalty stroke.'

'And then, on the short 13th, I took a 5-iron, well down the shaft.'

'No, sir, the Chief Constable lost a ball yesterday.'

CHAPTER FIVE

Women on the Links

The Moan of the Maiden

(After Tennyson)

Golf! Golf! Golf!
  By the side of the sounding sea;
And I would that my ears had never
  Heard aught of the 'links' and the 'tee'.

Oh, well for the man of my heart,
  That he bets on the 'holes' and the play
Oh, well for the 'caddie' that carries
  The 'clubs', and earns his pay.

He puts his red coat on,
  And he roams on the sandy hill;
But oh for the touch of that golfer's hand,
  That the 'niblick' wields with a will.

Golf! Golf! Golf!
  Where the 'bunkers' vex by the sea;
But the days of Tennis and Croquet
  Will never come back to me!

Mr Clarke
1.11.1890

Golf Victor!

Sir Golf and Sir Tennis are fighting like mad –
  Now Sir Tennis is blown, and Sir Golf's right above him,
And his face has a look that is weary and sad,
  As he hastily turns to the ladies, who love him,
But the racket falls from him, he totters, and swirls,
As he hears them cry, 'Golf is the game for the girls!'

Aunt Jubisca (pointing to earnest Golfer endeavouring to play out of quarry). 'DEAR ME, MAUD, WHAT A RESPECTABLY DRESSED MAN THAT IS BREAKING STONES!'

The girls crave for freedom, they cannot endure
   To be cramped up at Tennis in courts that are poky,
And they're all of them certainly, perfectly sure
   That they'll never again touch 'that horrible Croquet',
Where it's quite on the cards that they play with Papa,
And where all that goes on is surveyed by Mamma.

To Golf on the downs for the whole of the day
   Is 'so awfully jolly', they keep on asserting,
With a good-looking fellow to teach you the way,
   And to fill up the time with some innocent flirting,
And it may be the maiden is wooed and is won,
Ere the whole of the round is completed and done.

Henceforward, then, Golf is the game for the fair –
   At home, and abroad, or in pastures Colonial,
And the shouts of the ladies will quite fill the air
   For the Links that will turn into bonds Matrimonial,
And for husbands our daughters in future will seek
With the powerful aid of the putter and cleek!

Charles Geake
8.11.1890

A QUESTION OF FORM

Golfer. 'SHE'S A FINE WOMAN, ANDREW!'   *Andrew.* 'AY, SHE'S FINE THE NOO, BUT SHE GANGS A' TO PIECES IN THE RAIN.'

HOW MILITANT SUFFRAGETTES ARE MADE

Caddie (*to visitor*): 'THAT'S THE OLD GREEN TO THIS 'OLE, SIR. IT GETS FLOODED, SO THEY'VE GIVE IT TO THE LYDIES!'

Should Married Men be Allowed to Play Golf?

(*Extract from a Golfer's Diary*)

July 21. – Played ROBINSON, who would never win a match if it wasn't for his wife. Think that I shall start a links for bachelors only. (Mem. – Suggest to the committee that no married man is allowed to play golf in the mornings or afternoons.)

Hole I. I played perfectly, holing beautiful long putt. ROBINSON hopeless. One up.

Hole II. R. bunkered. Entirely his own fault. Two up.

Hole III. Holed my approach, allowing for both wind and slope of green; really a grand shot. Caught sight of Mrs R. as I walked to the next tee. Three up.

Hole IV. Thought that I might have to speak to Mrs R. at any minute. Missed my drive in consequence. Disgusting! Two up.

Hole V. R. seemed to be looking for his wife instead of attending to what I was saying. My drive lay on a buttercup, and who the deuce can be expected to play off buttercups? One up.

Hole VI. Stymied R. quite perfectly. He pretended to think that we were not playing stymies. We were. Two up.

Hole VII. Saw Mrs R. looking aimlessly out to sea. These loafing ladies are enough to put any man off his game. Why can't they do something? One up.

Hole VIII. R. may say what he likes, but he waved to his wife. I was also annoyed by his stockings, which I should think Mrs R. knitted. The sort of useless thing she would do. All square.

Hole IX. Got well away from Mrs R., and though my caddie coughed as I was approaching I laid my ball dead. Beautiful shot. One up at the turn.

Hole X. Had the hole in my pocket when R. laid his approach dead. Ridiculous luck. All square.

Hole XI. Just as I was driving I saw Mrs R. still looking at the sea. I complained, but R. took no notice. At any rate she cost me the hole. One down.

Hole XII. VARDON couldn't have played better than I did, and even R. had to say, 'Good shot!' twice. All square.

Hole XIII. As I was putting I had a feeling in my back that Mrs R. had arrived at last. Missed my putt and only halved the hole.

Hole XIV. Couldn't see Mrs R. anywhere. Wondered where on earth she had got to, or whether she was drowned. Of course I lost the hole. One down.

Hole XV. A little dispute, as R. claimed that his ball – which was under a wheelbarrow – was on ground under repair. Absolutely foolish, and I told him so. All square.

Hole XVI. Made a perfect drive, approach and putt. Looked everywhere for Mrs R. and couldn't see her. One up.

Hole XVII. Completely put off by wondering when I should see Mrs R. Most unfair. Told my caddie I should report him to the committee. All square.

Hole XVIII. Saw Mrs R. on a hill half a mile away. Got on my nerves. R. said, 'Halloa, there's my wife! I thought she wasn't coming out this morning.' Lost the hole and the match, and told the secretary that R.'s handicap ought to be reduced.

Turley Smith
25.7.1906

ACIDULATED GOLF

'DON'T KNOW HOW TO PLAY THIS, CADDIE?'
'WHY, YOU'VE GOT A GRAND LINE, SIR. FOLLOW THE S. THE OTHER GENTLEMAN'S BUNKERED IN THE E.'

The Passionate Golfer to his Love

Dearest, it almost breaks my heart
To speak the word that bids us part
   For ever past recall.
Were you less charming, had you less
Of that perfection in excess
   Which holds my soul in thrall,
I might dismiss you from my mind
At lucid intervals, and find
   My eye upon the ball.

Now, when I raise my club to drive
My well-meant efforts seldom thrive,
   Your presence seems too near.
No open champion, since the sky
Saw the first shaggy divot fly,
   The first bare patch appear,
Could at one time in rapture dwell
On all the charms you wield so well
   And also strike the sphere.

So when I'm playing through the green
The thought of all your grace, my queen,
   Intoxicates like wine.
'Witch'd by your beauty's mute appeal,
'Stead of the leathern grip, I feel
   Your tender hand in mine.
Then if I press, oh, who could blame?
Not Zeno's self, yet all the same
   The ball goes off the line.

But, ah! my cup of woe is full
When after socket, slice and pull
   Or fatuous half-topped roll,
Forth from the bunkers' grim embrace
With trembling lip and pallid face
   At last I near the hole –
Only to find, absorbed in you,
One cannot putt and worship too –
   Each needs a single soul!

So we must part; but not all grey
Will be your solitary way,
   For though our bonds I snap,
You'll watch as I relinquish fast
Stroke after stroke until at last
   I offer you, mayhap,
To dull the pain of parting thus
The privilege of seeing +
   Before my handicap!

P. B. Durnford
29.4.1908

Local Lady Champion (to member who has been pressed into service owing to a shortage of caddies).
'AWFULLY GOOD OF YOU TO CARRY FOR ME. YOU UNDERSTAND THE DIFFERENT CLUBS, DON'T YOU?'
Member. 'MY DEAR LADY, I UNDERSTAND THE WHOLE BAG OF TRICKS, BUT I CAN'T LIFT 'EM.'

Golf Enthusiast (on her return from following important match – ecstatically). 'OH, MOTHER! THE CHAMPION SPOKE TO ME!'
Mother. 'HOW INTERESTING, DEAR. WHAT DID HE SAY?'
Enthusiast. 'STAND ASIDE, THERE!'

Artist. 'SHE HAS A TOPPING HEAD, HASN'T SHE?'
Golfer. 'DON'T YOU THINK IT'S TEED A BIT TOO HIGH?'

HER FIRST MEDAL ROUND

Amelia (*to her putter*). 'HOW CAN YOU LOOK ME IN THE FACE AFTER THE WAY YOU LET ME DOWN TODAY?'

A Caddie of Comfort

She whispers when the ball is teed,
'Slow back, Sir, noo, and mind yer heid;
Just gie't a dunt and gar it speed;'
Yet, though it flies into the rough,
Declares I hit it right enough.

She says, when I have made a hash
Of every stroke and merely gash
Her native soil, 'Hoots! dinna fash!'
And when a two-foot putt goes skew,
'Yon's what the best o' them will do.'

Still, should I chance to keep the line
And manage the long hole in nine,
She tells me I am 'daein' fine,'
And then assures me with a laugh,
'Few will be givin' *you* a half!'

So at the many shots I've played
Most vilely she has simply said,
'Weel, Sir, no *every yin* is BRAID;'
Adding that even such as he
Have sometimes their bad days, like me.

Then, should I be, say, five holes down
And sure to lose my good half-crown,
She cries, 'Gang on! ye'll win the roun','
And, though defeated, she'll exclaim,
'Ye've seldom played a better game.'

And the next time I come to stay
She'll grip me by the hand and say,
'It's *far* too long ye've been away;'
So once again the ball is teed,
With 'Slow back, noo, and mind yer heid.'

F. G. Penney
4.5.1921

Colonel Pepper (to woman sauntering aimlessly across fairway). 'NOW THEN! HURRY UP WITH THAT BABY OF YOURS.'
Woman. 'BABY YOURSELF – PLAYING WITH THAT LITTLE BALL AND IN THEM KNICKERS!'

Neglected Wife (*to golf-fiend*). 'WHY NOT MAKE AN EFFORT AS YOU DID WITH YOUR SMOKING AND CUT IT DOWN TO ONE ROUND A DAY?'

Well-meaning Caddie. 'I CAN PUT YOU RIGHT, MISS; BUT, UNDERSTAND, YOU'LL 'AVE TO SIRRENDER YERSELF TO ME ABSLOOTLY.'

The Tigress. 'LET'S SEE – WHAT'S YOUR HANDICAP?'
The Rabbit. 'TWENTY-FOUR; BUT I'M FAIRLY BRIGHT OTHERWISE.'

THE LADY CHAMPION'S BALL: A ROMANCE OF THE LINKS.

THE LADY CHAMPION'S BALL: A ROMANCE OF THE LINKS.

'OFF TO GOLF AGAIN, JOHN? HAVE YOU FORGOTTEN THIS IS THE ANNIVERSARY OF OUR WEDDING?'
'BY JOVE, SO IT IS! AWFULLY GLAD YOU REMINDED ME, LITTLE WOMAN. I MUST TRY TO CELEBRATE IT WITH A REALLY GOOD ROUND.'

Professional (*at Indoor School of Golf*). 'ARE YOU GOING TO HAVE A LESSON, MADAM?'
Madam. 'NO; BUT MY FRIEND IS. I LEARNT LAST WEEK.'

First Player. 'MY WIFE THREATENS TO LEAVE ME IF I DON'T CHUCK GOLF.'
Second Player. 'THAT SOUNDS SERIOUS.'
First Player. 'IT *IS* SERIOUS. I SHALL MISS HER.'

Wife (accompanying dud golfer for the first time). 'THIS CLUB IS FAR TOO EXPENSIVE, LESLIE. I'VE CALCULATED THAT IT COSTS YOU ABOUT SEVEN-AND-SIXPENCE EVERY TIME YOU TRY TO HIT THE BALL.'

'Well, how did the big golf match go . . .?'

'Would you ladies mind moving out of earshot, please?'

'It's just like billiards.'

'I'm two up!'

'Then guess what . . . he topped it into a bunker!'

'The others seem to be getting on much faster.'

'Somewhere in between the Scilla campanulata and the Oxalis deppei.'

'I love your straight left arm, your pivot, your wrist-snap . . .'

'Now, Mr Grimdyke, you're just not concentrating on the
overlapping grip.'

'Oh, God – not **another** moral victory.'

'Promise when we're married you won't spend half your time on the golf course?'

'What was the word the doctor said I said while I was under the anaesthetic?'

'Can't I plead with you, Helen? It isn't my wish that our
marriage should end like this.'

CHAPTER SIX

Kit

The Lucky Golf-Ball

'Buy a ball, Sir?'

I turned quickly and observed one of those unhappy beings that wander dispiritedly over our golf-courses, poking about among the clumps of gorse and heather that offer so secure a sanctuary to the hard-pressed golf-ball. To quote the words of Polcastle, one of our committee, it is in the worst possible form to purchase a foundling ball from one of these wretches; it simply is not done by members of a decent club.

'Certainly not,' I said brusquely, turning to contemplate my lie, an execrable one.

'It's a very *lucky* ball, Sir.'

I paused to regard more closely the depressing figure that had appeared as from nowhere without a sound. He was tall, lean and elderly, dressed in black from head to foot, in a thread-bare tail-coat and a dilapidated bowler hat. His features were gaunt and lugubrious, but in his penetrating eyes shone a curious glint that checked the angry exclamation on my lips. For a brief instant a strange and eerie atmosphere seemed to hover about his lank form, and I felt an uncomfortable shiver run down my spine.

'What do you mean – a lucky ball?' I demanded.

'It is an exceptionally lucky ball, Sir,' he replied. 'I am sure you will find it brings you good fortune. Only sixpence, Sir – a tanner, as we commonly say.'

I hesitated. A recollection of Polcastle standing with feet apart delivering a lecture to an eighteen-handicap man flashed into my mind and decided me. I hastily fished out sixpence.

'I shall expect something very extraordinary from this,' I said with an uneasy laugh.

He gravely lifted his hat and bowed. 'You will not be disappointed, Sir,' he said. 'Allow me to thank you, on my own behalf and for all my brother unfortunates who wander so miserably upon these links. Think kindly of them, Sir; think charitably of them, and good luck will not fail to attend you.'

I heard Simpson calling impatiently from the other side of the fairway and, seizing my mashie, I played out; then I turned again to question the remarkable creature at my side.

He had vanished as silently and as mysteriously as he had come.

On the next tee I selected my newly acquired ball. I am not a good, at least not a reliable, driver. I hit the ball forcibly enough, but the direction it takes not infrequently causes me surprise and disappointment. They tell me it is something I do with my left foot. I believe I lift it too high in the air.

I addressed the ball and drove. Straight and true it sped down the middle of the fairway – a superb, a perfect drive.

'Good *shot!*' exclaimed Simpson with ill-concealed astonishment.

I would like, if I had time, to describe the rest of the round to you stroke by stroke; to illustrate in detail how I did the short fourteenth in two after pitching on the roof of a shelter, and the long seventeenth in four. Enough to say that I won every remaining hole.

Next day I went round in eighty-one, and on the following Saturday I won the monthly medal with a net score of fifty-six. The great

Small Scot. 'LOOK, FAYTHER – A NEW GOWF-BA' AH FOUND; LOST ON THE LINKS.'
Father. 'ARE YE SURE IT WAS LOST, ANGUS?'
Small Scot. 'OO AY. AH SAW THE MANNIE AN' HIS CADDIE LOOKIN' FOR IT.'

Heathcote, a scratch player, came and congratulated me personally.

It is difficult for me to describe my pleasurable sensations of the days that followed. The thwarted desires and vicious complexes that embitter the soul of the mediocre player were lifted from me. My personality seemed to expand and the world became a blither place; a livelier emerald twinkled, as it were, on the greens. Members nudged one another as I passed.

Only the objectionable Polcastle remained aloof and scornful. 'Don't tell me,' I heard him sneeringly remark, 'that a man who waves his left foot in the air is a golfer. He'll come a cropper before long; they always do.'

My great chance came when I had to meet him in the final of the General Bufflethwaite Cup, the event of our club year. Polcastle was openly and contemptuously confident. For myself, I lovingly caressed my precious ball and smiled; with this powerful ally I would humble my arrogant opponent to the dust.

The final of the Bufflethwaite is played over thirty-six holes, but I have not the heart now to tell you much about the match. At the end of the morning round I was three up, and when we came to the tenth tee in the afternoon I had established the commanding lead of eight holes. My drive hummed crisply down the fairway; Polcastle sliced badly over a tree.

In grim silence we tramped together to look for his ball. Then, as Polcastle stood contemplating a peculiarly awkward lie, a weedy youth in a tattered jacket emerged from behind a bush and shuffled towards me.

PLUS AND MINUS FOURS.

'Buy a ball, Sir?' he whined.

Polcastle looked up with a savage exclamation. The vagrant's eyes sought mine appealingly. But the dominating presence of Polcastle overawed me and my courage oozed away.

'Certainly not,' I snapped; 'be off with you.'

He slunk away without a word.

Polcastle recovered with an heroic effort and I went to play my second. But both my conscience and my nerve were affected and I pulled the shot. Nevertheless it cleared the obstructions and looked to pitch on open ground. If my good fortune held I might still win, or at least halve the hole. But when we reached the spot not a trace of the ball could be seen. There was not a bush, scarcely a tuft of grass, that could have concealed it. And suddenly, on a distant fairway, stark against the evening sky, I descried a lank figure in a black tail-coat hastening over the brow of the hill with swift determined strides.

I dropped my clubs with an exclamation of dismay. 'Hi!' I cried. 'Stop! Come back!'

'What the blazes is the matter with you?' demanded Polcastle.

'That man,' I shouted, 'look – he's taken my ball.'

'Don't be a fool,' snarled Polcastle; 'how could he possibly have touched your ball?'

Already the ominous figure had disappeared behind the hill, and I knew pursuit was useless. With despair in my heart I abandoned the hole.

From this point the match degenerated, as far as I was concerned, into a humiliating farce. Never have I played such abject golf or been pursued by such persistent ill-fortune. Polcastle won the Cup at the eighteenth after I had thrice driven out of bounds.

'You'll never play golf till you learn to keep that left foot on the ground,' was his only comment.

Morose and dejected I sat alone in a corner of the smoke-room. Simpson (somehow I had not been seeing much of Simpson lately) approached me. 'Bad luck, old man,' he said gruffly; 'you struck a rotten patch. Walking down?'

Without a word I rose and together we left the club-house. Outside it was dark, and as we passed through the avenue of trees that leads to the road a shape of intenser blackness seemed to detach itself from the surrounding shadows, and I felt rather than heard a reproachful voice speaking in my ear.

'You disappointed me, Sir,' it said. 'I would never have failed you if you had not failed us.'

Simpson struck a match to light his pipe, and in the flickering gleam I saw a lugubrious countenance regarding me from the shadows with dark accusing eyes.

I leapt forward to grapple with it, bumped into a tree and reeled back bruised and breathless.

'Hello, what's up?' inquired Simpson.

'See,' I cried, 'the creature in black! Quick! Don't let him get away.'

'Come, pull yourself together, old boy,' said Simpson kindly. 'You've been having a couple too many at the nineteenth.' He came up and took my arm.

C. L. M. Brown
4.4.1928

The Golfer's Game-Book

I have always been struck by the fact that no enterprising publishing house has ever put on the market for the benefit of mankind a Golfer's Game-Book. Such a publication, and I am taking steps to shake someone up about it, should be designed on the lines of an elaborate sporting game-book, with a page set aside for each round. I am sure that to anyone who can tolerate such a thing as golfers' introspection it would supply a long-felt want.

Last week I went so far as to get a good-natured printer to rough me out some specimen pages, a couple of which I promptly took round to old Colonel Hackitt, of Blank File Cottage, to see if he would give them an airing. As methodical as a sewing-machine, the Colonel in his lonely retirement still retains a soldierly love of making notes, tabulating things and filling up forms. I couldn't have gone to a better man.

Four days later a registered envelope arrived with the following letter:–

SIR, – Your forms (unnumbered, two) are returned herewith duly completed and for your further attention.

I have the honour to be, Sir,

Your obedient Servant,

GEORGE C. HACKITT,

Lieut.-Col.

Here is the first:–

Name of Club.   Trudgett Magna.

Date.   8th November, 1931. Morning.

Opponent.   That swine Maltby.

Weather.   Abominable.

Wind.   Always in my face.

Notes on Course.   A rabbit-warren.

Notes on Club-house.   Like a third-class pub.

People introduced to.   Lots of cads who either tried to sell me coal or make me take out insurance policies.

Good Shots.   None.

Noticeable Faults.   A tendency to knot myself just below the knees.

New stories heard.   Some feeble jest about receptive bunkers, of which I couldn't see the point.

Strokes taken.   107.

Result of Match.   Lost on the last green.

Frank statement as to how I played, to be signed by opponent.   He played the game of his life. – (*Signed*) J. V. M. (There is a note here in the Colonel's handwriting: 'A damn lie.')

This is the second one:–

Name of Club.   Trudgett Magna.

Date.   8th November, 1931. Afternoon.

Opponent.   Major Sir J. Vernon Maltby, D.S.O.

Weather. Ideal.

Wind. None that I noticed.

Notes on the Course. Excellent. Greens superb, especially the eighteenth, where I holed a seven-yard putt.

Notes on Club-house. Very comfortable; fairway to the nineteenth well laid out.

People introduced to. Fear I rather misjudged them this morning; really a very decent lot.

Good Shots. Every one, nearly.

Noticeable Faults. No recollection of any.

New stories heard. Tale about a man who couldn't putt. I forget it, but it was frightfully funny.

Strokes taken. 107.

Result. Won on the last green.

Frank statement as to how I played, to be signed by opponent. Maltby was too bad-tempered to sign, but honestly I played the game of my life.

And now, please, will any publisher take over this child of mine? It's going cheap.

George C. Nash
11.11.1931

Gentlemen v. Players

'The hill-climbing power of a Cushman Champion Electric lets you take steep hills straight up where other cars must travel on the bias. Add to the time-proven, trouble-free engineering, the fine modern styling of the Cushman, and you see why this is the most popular golf car on the course today.'

'The Fort Knox Putter – Made of fourteen-karat gold, designed by a leading jeweler. $200 to $1,000. Hess Bros., Allentown, Pa.'

'Hooch Handle – Fine golf umbrella has a special handle that unscrews to reveal flask.' – *Esquire* advertisements

The parking-attendant at the third tee waved the four golf-cars into line; the drivers drew up, and switched off. Above them, a faint blue petrol-haze hung in the still air.

'Man!' said Hummer. 'What a day! What heat!'

'Yeah,' said Sorfik, in the car beside him. 'Howja manage to stay alive innat goddam beancan? Whyncha get with the crowd and pick up one of these open jobs?'

Belt, in the third car, leaned forward and turned off his radio.

'They ain't so hot,' he said. 'Comes a sudden shower, where's ya protection? A guy could catch pneumonia.' He flicked a switch, and a small plastic hood snapped over his car. The others could see him inside, smiling.

Fender's caddy jumped out, and ran round to open his master's door. Fender strolled across to his partners. He ran a finger along Belt's coachwork, and shouted through the plastic top.

'TIN! It's all tin, Belt!' He waved at his own car. 'Steel chassis, Italian styling, real

excitedly. 'Hold on, fellas, this ya haveta see!' He ran back to his car.

'Not my taste at all,' said Fender, quietly, to Belt. 'Flashy. Me, I like a good Harris Tweed outfit. Imported.' He showed Belt the label.

'Nice,' said Belt. 'But it's ninety inna shade. Aintcha uncomfortable?'

Fender screwed up his face, and sweatdrops scuttled down the new wrinkles. 'What's this "uncomfortable" jazz? I'm playing *golf*, fella, or didja forget? Suppose I meet someone onna links, a business competitor, or something –

'Mind if I play through? I've got a slow puncture.'

imitation-pigskin seats, automatic transmo, air-conditioner. Imported. Whatsa guy in your position doing inna bugtrap like this?'

Belt got out sheepishly.

'Din't know they was on the market. This month's *Esquire* din't get here yet.'

The four players walked six yards to the tee, mopping their faces. Hummer looked at Sorfik approvingly.

'*Those*,' he said, 'I like. The mohair plus-fours. Style!'

'I gotta nanorak to match,' said Sorfik

you want me to look like a tramp?'

He selected an alligator-handled driver and sent his ball sixty yards down the fairway; his caddy ran up, and brushed the fragments of divot from Fender's coat.

'Gotta good boy there,' said Sorfik.

'The best,' said Fender fiercely. 'Scotch. Imported. Say something, Angus.'

'It's a braw, bricht, moonlicht nicht, tonicht,' said the caddy.

'Fantastic!' cried Hummer. 'The genuine article.'

'I've always had coloureds,' said Belt, grudgingly. 'You know where you are with the coloureds.'

He swung his club, cut a black swathe in the turf, and knocked the ball a dozen yards away.

'Goddam balls cost a buck apiece,' muttered Belt. 'You'd think they could turn out a decent ball for a buck.'

Fender looked at him stonily. 'Without a sealskin inner shell, you're nothing,' he said. 'Buck eighty-five.'

The three drove off noisily in their cars, leaving Belt to try again. This time, his ball went a clear seventy yards. He ran happily to his car, leapt in, and roared off.

'What kepcha?' asked Fender. 'Me and the boys was talking about holidays.'

'I just got back from Palm Springs,' said Hummer proudly. 'Nine courses. Swimming pools. Night-clubs. Jet from LA takes forty minutes.'

'It took me two hours in the helicopter,' said Belt. 'But it's cosier.'

Sorfik was making a casual study of his lizardskin golf-shoes.

'You all gotta come round some night, see the movie I shot at the Royal and Ancient,' he said. They were silent, so he glanced up. 'It's a European golf-course. I got colour-slides, too.'

'Where did *you* go?' said Belt to Fender.

'Capri.' Hummer and Belt looked respectful. Sorfik hesitated.

'Good links?' he asked levelly.

'Private,' snapped Fender. 'Ordinary tourists don't get to play. I got these Wop business associates. With a château.'

Sorfik slashed at his ball; it sliced away from him, bounced off a tree, hit the roof of a passing golf-car, and rolled into a bunker. Silently, he changed into Grecian sandals, and drove away. They watched him vanish into the pit.

'A bad loser,' said Hummer.

'Yeah,' said Fender. 'Some sportsman!'

They teed up, and got sixty yards nearer the green; Belt wiped his brow ostentatiously, and cried: 'Waddya say to a drink, fellas?'

Before they could reply, he had unscrewed the handle of his golf umbrella and withdrawn a flask. He offered them plastic containers shaped like golfballs.

'Pretty cute, huh? Here, take some bourbon.'

Hummer unscrewed his own umbrella. 'I prefer Scotch.'

Chastened, Belt turned to Fender, only to find him watching his caddy decant the liquor from two golf-umbrellas into the shaft of a fake Number Three iron. Fender sipped.

'Too much vermouth,' he said.

Since all that could be seen of Sorfik was an astrakhan deerstalker bobbing above a cloud of sand, the three went off without him. A few yards short of the green, however, Hummer fell prey to a party of four hysterical women in a DAR Golfibus who ignored a 'Halt – Fairway Ahead' sign, and rammed him amidships. Fender and Belt did not wait for the ambulance; there was little that anyone could do for Hummer.

'Should've had a steel chassis,' said Fender, selecting a club. The caddy handed him his Fort Knox Putter, and giving the shot plenty of wrist, so that the gold faces glinted in the sun, he hammered the ball past the hole and off the green.

Belt took his Klondike eighteen-karat Special, and sank the putt. Fender glowered at him.

'Guess that diamond thumb-mark really helps,' said Belt amiably.

'Lemme see!' Fender whipped an eye-glass from its doeskin pouch, squinted at Belt's club, and hurled it down triumphantly.

'I thought so!' he cried. 'A rhinestone! They conned you with a lousy rhinestone.'

Belt set his jaw.

'Those sons-of-bitches!' He lowered his voice, and unwound the polarised golf-glasses from his face. 'I wouldn't like this to get out, old buddy. Round the clubhouse, know what I mean?'

'Count on me,' said Fender. 'But I don't see how I can give you the hole.'

Belt rubbed the golden club against his chin, frowning.

'I guess you're right,' he said. 'My lousy luck. Still – you can't win 'em all.'

'Don't take it bad,' said Fender, marking his card. 'It's all in the game.'

Alan Coren
26.6.1963

on

Motorised
Golf

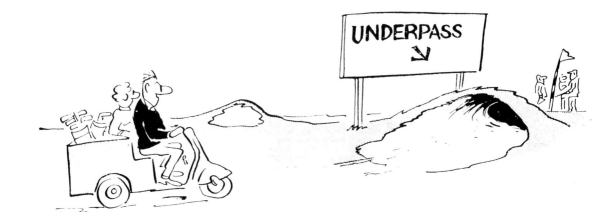

UNDERPASS

'We're incompatible.'

*'It's a Spalding No. 7, but I don't think it's **my** Spalding No. 7.'*

CHAPTER SEVEN

Ploys and Gambits

The Golfing Brain

My reason for relating this story is partly that I am unable to get to sleep and partly that I have a queer feeling it may be of some slight help to the many who share with me the misfortune of being terribly bad at golf. As to its effect upon my own future I dare not yet begin to speculate.

It was in the evening of another good Sunday gone wrong. I reclined in a deck-chair beside the eighteenth green, pondering sadly on the doings of the day, wondering if there was anything I could possibly do about my golf beyond the fruitless questioning of my caddie as to what I was doing wrong; whether it was possible that I could be doomed to a state of lifelong rabbitry, and whether, after all, I should not be far, far happier if I spent my Sundays in future in a more Christian-like manner, mowing my lawn, trimming my hedge and playing stump cricket in the garden with Jack and Jill.

A stranger came up to me, carrying a bag of clubs, and, almost as if he had read my thoughts, he remarked, 'Has it ever occurred to you, Sir, how strange it is that there should be such a difference between different men's golf?'

'It has,' I replied. 'Curiously enough I was thinking about it at this very moment.'

'Why is it,' he asked, 'that some men swing out freely at the ball, making a delicious cracking noise when the club head meets it, while others stroke at it in an apologetic sort of way,

making a noise like something dropping on to a Turkey carpet? Funny, isn't it?'

'It is not altogether funny,' I sighed.

'But it *is* funny,' he insisted. 'Do you know why it is?'

I felt a little irritated by this question. It was the very one I had been struggling in vain to answer for years and years.

'I can't tell you,' I replied. 'Practice, I suppose – and strength and eye.'

'Practice?' he said. 'My dear Sir, lots of men play golf regularly and never look like getting into practice. And as for strength and eye – why, a little man in spectacles may quite well destroy an ex-champion; and many a hefty body contains a heart that has gone all flabby with consistent failure on the links.'

This was true. I made no reply.

'Yes,' he went on, 'and the astonishing thing is that so few people realise why it is.'

'Does anyone?' I asked.

'Of course,' he replied. 'The difference between hitting a golf-ball well and hitting it abominably is nothing else but the difference between two habits of mind – the habit of deciding to do so and the habit of deciding not to.'

I looked at him in surprise. He appeared to be quite serious.

'You see,' he added quietly, 'it cannot possibly be anything else.'

'But the swing?' I said. 'You're allowing nothing for the swing.'

'The swing,' he answered, 'is the very thing I am talking about. You don't suppose that arms and legs and heads and wrists have some

HOLIDAY PUTTS

MR PUNCH'S ADVICE TO THOSE WHO FIND THEMSELVES 'OFF'
THIS BRANCH OF THE GAME.

mysterious power of self-movement, without any direction from the brain? You don't suppose that it is just a difference in the construction of men's limbs which causes some men to drive two-hundred-and-fifty yards down the middle of the fairway and others to flop their ball miserably into the heather?'

'No,' I agreed. 'It does not seem likely. And yet –'

'Yet what?' he inquired.

'I was thinking about myself,' I said.

'Quite so,' he replied. 'Why do you not drive a fine long ball down the middle and put all your iron shots on the green?'

'I assure you,' I returned with some heat, 'it is not because I have decided not to do so. I am not the world's worst golfer from choice.'

'Pardon me,' he said gently, 'but you are wrong. It does not occur to you to hit at a golf-ball as if you were the world's best golfer. That is where you fail.'

'Indeed it does,' I told him. 'It occurs to me whenever I've happened to play a couple of decent holes. I stand up on the next tee brimful of confidence, waggle freely, swing well out – and dribble the ball painfully into the rough twenty yards ahead.'

'Exactly,' he replied. 'But that has nothing to do with the habit of deciding to hit the ball. That is the habit of thinking backwards – of deciding that, as you've just played a couple of decent holes, you can slash out in a senseless and abandoned manner at the next one. Now, if you hit the ball perfectly every time——'

'Don't be silly,' I said impatiently; and I got up from my chair.

'Wait!' he cried. 'Stay where you are!' He pulled a driver out of his bag. 'Take this club,' he said.

There was a ring of authority in his voice and I felt compelled to obey. I took the club from his hand. He knelt down on the ground and teed up a ball; and I waited for further instructions.

'Now then,' he commanded, 'you are to hit that ball. You will not pinch in your arms and check the head of the club just at the moment when it should be travelling at full speed. Nor will you toss your head up in the air like a man in an agony of distress. You will stand up comfortably, swing freely, rhythmically and sensibly, and you will hit that ball as far as a golf-ball can be hit.'

As he spoke a curious sensation of power came tingling through my frame; it was as if I had been hypnotised – transferred in one instant from a rabbit to a tiger. I fell straight into an easy stance, swung my arms gloriously behind me and let out at the ball with every ounce of strength in my body.

It was a magnificent exhilarating feeling, such a feeling as I had never before known in my life. Away went the ball – far over the big bunker that crosses the fairway of the eighteenth – on, on towards the tee, almost out of sight. For some seconds I stood, like a statue of VARDON, watching its flight over my right shoulder; and when I unwound myself I found that my friend had teed up another ball in its place.

'Again!' he cried.

And again I hit out with the same supreme confidence and easy force; and again the ball sped far, far away on its course – even further than the first one, and straight as a dart all the way.

'Again!' he cried – five, ten, I know not how many times, and each time the ball travelled further and further, until at length, maddened with joy, my whole being afire with the lust of hitting, I made that last grand stupendous shot. Never as long as I live shall I forget that shot. Away sped the ball – far away over the bunker, over the ditch beyond, over the road, over the railway embankment, over the trees in my own garden, through the open window of my bedroom, slap on to the electric reading-lamp which stands on the table beside my bed. It was a moment of moments, hectic, colossal, indescribable. But it has passed. . . .

I have rescued the reading-lamp from the floor and put it back on its table – but, alas! I shall never find that ball.

L. B. Gullick
8.7.1925

AN ILLUSTRATED CONJUGATION.

TO DRIVE: – VERB – IRREGULAR – ACTIVE & NEUTER.

He Drives

She drives

It drives

I will drive

That I may drive

About to drive

Driving

Having driven

It is not driven

YOU WILL NOT DRIVE –

YOU SHOULD DRIVE –

THEY ARE DRIVING

IT *SHALL* BE DRIVEN

WILL YOU DRIVE?

I HAVE DRIVEN!

YOU DROVE!

DID YOU DRIVE?

LET THEM DRIVE!

THE FINISHES OF THE FAMOUS

A Politician.

A Novelist.

An Actor.

A Scientist.

A Welfare Worker.

A Painter.

A General.

A Footballer.

A Film-Star.

Conversation Golf

'Marvellous air one gets up here,' said the man.

'Is it?' said I.

The air was absolutely foul.

'That's a sparrow-hawk hovering,' said the man, pointing to some nasty spot in the sky.

'Very possibly,' I replied with hauteur. I did not care if it was a boiled owl.

'How plainly one can see France!' said the man. 'You can almost pick out the buildings on the other side.'

'Mph,' I said.

We are an island people, I believe. We are becoming, I hope, more British every day. At a moment of national emergency such as the present it ill becomes us to simulate curiosity about a country that not only tries to dump luxuries in our ports but actually remains on the Gold Standard. Clearly the man was a cad.

I knew of course the game he was playing, or trying to play – the usual game played by a stranger whom one picks up at a strange club. He was a middle-aged man, hard-bitten (at least I hope so) and wearing a yellow pullover. With a lucky lead of one hole he meant to consolidate his advantage by boosting the atmosphere. At two up he tried to clinch his success by disgusting references to ornithology. Three to the good, he became a mere anti-patriot, hoping to snatch a cheap victory by posing as a cosmopolitan *flâneur*. But I bided my hour.

I holed a long putt on the fourth green for a half. That shook him visibly.

'How delightful the thyme smells!' was the best he could do.

I had noticed some kind of objectionable odour myself, but I refused to admit the fact. I had earned the right to put in a counter-blow and I had laid my plan of campaign.

'Queer sort of political situation,' I said as we walked to the fifth tee, 'hunting for formulas like this.'

It was good enough. He sliced badly into the long grass, while I went down the centre of the fairway. I rested for a few moments, picking out houses in France or wherever it was, while he and his caddie hunted for their formula. They did not find it.

I determined to play a cool and wary game after this. There was much that I might have said as he came up moist and blasphemous to the sixth. I had seen a dead seagull, for instance, but I said nothing about it, and there was a German liner standing close into shore. It is not the best policy to hammer your opponent too heavily at the start and provoke unlimited reprisals. I preferred to stick to my original line. I merely asked him how he thought the North of England would vote as a whole on the policy of Protection, and the ruse availed. He made a noise like an ailing cow and topped into a bunker, though the wind, smelling strongly of thyme, was at his back.

But he was not without resources and, gaining a short hole by pointing out the autumnal tints in the woods, he was still two up at the turn. I won the long tenth by alluding to bi-metallism, but he pulled me back again at the eleventh, and had the insufferable audacity at the twelfth tee to ask me whether I had seen the Roman remains at Richborough. I had, but if he thought he could make me scoop my drive by alluding to a lot of miserable rubbish left here by the troops of CLAUDIUS he was mistaken, and I soon proved it to him. I laid my approach as dead as the Emperor HONORIUS and stood one down. I should have been level with him at the next if the mouldy air of the Downs, with its vile scent of thyme, had not blown my ball off the green; and he increased his advantage by driving almost sixty yards nearer France than I did, which filled him obviously with overweening pride.

It was a moment for dispensing with tradition. He had the honour and was opening his mouth, probably to make some coarse remark about botany which would have ruined my back-swing, when I took the game into my own hands.

'It's a difficult situation,' I said to him, smiling pleasantly, 'but the old country is not dead yet.'

He stared open-mouthed. He could hardly believe his ears. I don't suppose any opponent had ever been three holes down to him in all his hard-bitten, yellow-pullovered life on the fifteenth tee and had the nerve to come up cool and smiling with a remark about politics just before the drive. The wind was out of his sails.

THE MAN WHO BELIEVED IN THE FOLLOW-THROUGH.

'What d'you mean?' he said.

'Just what I say,' I answered. 'It's an awkward situation, but I do really think that with a National Government we shall all of us pull through.'

He did, anyway. Right into the little spinney on the left. Very likely it was full of sparrow-hawks. It took him five shots to get to the green. So ruffled was he that I took the next two holes with a mere reference to Mr PHILIP SNOWDEN's peerage and the curious position of Mr LLOYD GEORGE, the first of which made him fluff a mashie pitch and the second socket an iron.

Clearly the drama at the eighteenth was bound to be intense. We walked with set faces to the tee, each of us searching in his mind for the death-blow. Very suddenly there was an awful noise overhead.

'That must be the air-mail,' said the man.

I doubt if a more dastardly attack has ever been delivered. In a fey moment I might have looked up at the wretched thing. But I held my ground.

'I don't think it was,' I said. 'I think it was a wheatear.'

Then I drove. It was a fairly decent one. He searched in his pocket for his peg tee.

'We must all press forward,' I said, 'against the ranks of Squandermania.'

He drove. It went about sixty-five yards. I had a putt in hand and won. I thank the PRIME MINISTER for it.

E. V. Knox
14.10.1931

MR AND MRS TOPHAM MAKE A RESOLUTION NEVER TO 'LOOK UP' IN 1930.

Lifemanship

Gamesmanship Research

It is our purpose here to summarise some of the recent findings of the Gamesmanship Research Committee. Thousands of people, or certainly scores, have sent in their recommendations for new gamesploys and gambits. Our task is to sift, and to co-ordinate.

A SUMMARY OF RECENT WORK ON GOLFMANSHIP

Always remember that it is in golf that the skilful gamesman can bring his powers to bear most effectively. The constant companionship of golf, the cheery contact, means that *you are practically on top* of your opponent, at his elbow. The novice, therefore, will be particularly susceptible to your gambits.

Remember the basic rules. Remember the possibilities of defeat by tension. Gamesmen are aware of the 'Flurry', as it is called, in relation to lawn tennis. *It is an essential part of Winning Golf.* The atmosphere, of course, is worked up long before the game begins.

Your opponent is providing the car. You are a little late. You have forgotten something. Started at last, suggest that 'Actually we ought to get rather a move on – otherwise we may miss our place.'

'What place?' says the opponent.

'Oh, well, it's not a bad thing to be on the first tee on time.' Though no time has been fixed Opponent will soon be driving a little fast, a little tensely, and after you have provided one minor misdirection he arrives at the clubhouse taut.

In the locker room one may call directions to an invisible steward or non-existent timekeeper. 'We ought to be off at 10.38.' 'Keep it going for us,' and so forth.

OPPONENT. Who's that you're shouting to?

GAMESMAN. Oh, it's only the Committee man for starting times.

Your opponent will be rattled, and be mystified, too, if he comes out to find the course practically empty.

If for some reason it happens to be full you can put into practice Crowded Coursemanship, and suggest, before every other shot

Opponent plays, that 'We mustn't take too long – otherwise we shall have to signal that lunatic Masterman, behind us, to come through. Then we're sunk.'

Here are some notes on certain general gamesmanship plays, in their relation to golf.

Mixed Foursomes

In a mixed foursome it is important in the basic foursome play (*i.e.*, winning the admiration of your opponent's female partner) that your own drive should be longer than that of the opposing man, who will, of course, be playing off the same tee as yourself.

Should he possess definite superiority in length you must either (*a*) be 'dead off my drive, for some reason' all day – a difficult position to maintain throughout eighteen holes; (*b*) say 'I'm going to stick to my spoon off the tee,' and drive with a Fortescue's Special Number 3 – an ordinary driver dis-

←— WIND

F WILSON

WHO WERE THE GAMESWOMEN OF 1905?

Miss Christabel Pritt is said to have won the Newfoundland Vase, played that year in a gale, by the superior clothesmanship of her 'Breeze' hat grip. Happy days, when such aids could be bought for $3\frac{1}{2}d$.

guised to look like a spoon, and named 'spoon' in large letters on the surface of the head; (c) use the Frith-Morteroy counter.

The general play in mixed foursomes, however, differs widely from the Primary Gambits of a men's four. But beginners often feel the lack of a cut-and-dried guide.

In the all-male game, of course, when A and B are playing against C and D, the usual thing, if all is going well, is for A and B to be on delightfully good terms with each other, a model of easy friendship and understanding. Split Play is only brought into play by the A-B partnership if C-D look like becoming 2 up. A then makes great friends with C, and is quietly sympathetic when D, C's partner, makes the suspicion of an error, until C is not very unwillingly brought to believe that he is carrying the whole burden. His dislike for D begins to show plainly. D should soon begin to play really badly.

In the mixed game all is different. *Woo the opposing girl* is the rule. To an experienced mixed-man like Du Carte the match is a microcosm of the whole panorama of lovers' advances.

He will start by a series of tiny services, microscopic considerations. The wooden tee picked up, her club admired, the 'Is that chatter bothering you?' The whole thing done with suggestions, just discernible, that her own partner is a little insensitive to these courtlinesses, and that if only *he* were her partner what a match they'd make of it.

Du Carte, meanwhile, would be annoying the opposing man, by saying that 'Golf is only an excuse for getting out into the country. The average male is shy of talking about his love for birds and flowers. But isn't that . . . after all——'

Du Carte was so loathsome to his male friends at such moments that they became over-anxious to win the match. Whereas the female opponent, on the contrary, was beginning to feel that golf was not perhaps so important as sympathetic understanding.

By the twelfth hole Du Carte was able to suggest, across the distance of the putting green, that he was fast falling in love. And by the crucial sixteenth Female Opponent would have been made to feel not only that Du Carte

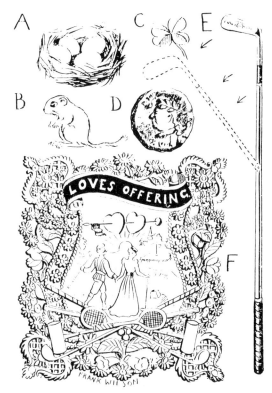

GAMESMANSHIP ACCESSORIES LTD

We supply amusing aids to Natural History ploy or Sussexmanship, *e.g.*,

(A) A nest with unbreakable eggs attached. This can be carried in the bag and placed surreptitiously near your opponent's lie in the rough. A discussion *breaking the flow* of his game can easily be extemporised. Easier to carry perhaps is

(B) 'The wee tim'rous beastie' (R. Burns). This can be supplied asleep.

(C) DEHYDRATED FOUR-LEAF CLOVER for presenting to the female opponent in a MIXED FOURSOME. Only needs wetting before the match and is then carried in damp blotting paper.

(D) ROMAN COIN. Supplied with synthetic moss or rust. Very lifelike. Discussion as to when there were Roman encampments on the golf course follows discovery. Could be presented to a lady to be made into a brooch.

(E) We supply No. 4 iron, hinged in the centre of the shaft. Use as follows: when opponent has reduced your lead to all square, it is easy to make it appear that you are breaking this club across your knee, remarking meanwhile that 'you are never going to play golf again.' Then return club to bag and play steadily.

(F) VALENTINE, for presentation to woman opponent in foursome.

Note. – We also supply dead bird for dropping near feet of female opponent in order to induce emotions incompatible with the winning vein.

had offered a proposal of marriage but that she, shyly and regretfully, had refused him.

Du Carte invariably won these matches two and one. For he knew the First Law of Mixed Gamesmanship: that *No woman can refuse a man's offer of marriage and beat him in match play at the same time.*

The Left Hand–Right Hand Play

I believe it was O. Sitwell who devised this simple rule for play against left-handers. If (as so often happens) your opponent, though left-handed in games generally, yet plays golf with ordinary right-hand clubs, it is a good thing, during the first hole *after the fifth* which he plays badly, to say:

SELF.   Do you mind if I say something?

L.H.   No. What?

SELF.   Have you ever had the feeling that you are *playing against the grain?*

L.H.   No – how do you mean?

SELF.   Well, you're really left-handed, aren't you?

L.H.   I certainly am – except for golf.

SELF.   Have you ever been tempted to make the big change?

L.H.   How do you mean?

SELF.   Play golf left-handed as well. Chuck those clubs away. Fling them into the bonfire. Damn the expense – and get a brand-new set of left-handed clubs.

L.H.   Yes, but——

SELF.   *You know* that is your natural game. Be extravagant.

L.H.   It isn't the expense——

SELF.   Money doesn't mean anything nowadays anyhow.

L.H.   I mean——

SELF.   Everybody's income's the same, really.

The fact that your opponent has been advised to play right-handedly by the best professional in the country will make him specially anxious to prove by his play that you are in the wrong. The usual results follow. If he is not only a left-hander but plays with left-handed clubs as well the same conversation will do, substituting the word *right* for *left* where necessary.

Stephen Potter
15.11.1950

'On the other hand, Bobby Locke says . . .'

Books are There to Help

This time I am going to hit my drive properly, and I shall do it the simple way. What on earth's the point of reading all these clever tips if you don't use them?

I am standing in a barrel which reaches to my waist. The barrel is wider than my shoulders, but will narrow proportionately as the club's loft increases, reaching shoulder-width with a 5-iron. My feet touch the sides. A railway line runs straight from the barrel and me to the pin, where the tracks meet. The ball is teed up on one rail. I place my feet on the other. Between the bottom of the peg's cup and the far rail is an unused cheque book. The peg goes through the cheque book and no daylight is showing.

I am standing in a barrel on a railway line.

In my left hand I now hold a pitcher of water. From the back of this hand a piece of string stretches towards the pin above and parallel to the near rail. I fold the right hand over the left thumb with the pressure of a friendly handshake.

I am standing in a barrel on a railway line with string sprouting from the back of my left hand, congratulating myself on carrying a pitcher of water.

The club properly gripped, I take up my stance. With my feet still on the near rail, I sit on a shooting stick. From the right ankle downwards I am a pigeon; from the left downwards Charlie Chaplin. I wear heavy-rimmed spectacles, a plumb line drops from my chin to a point on the rail an inch to the left of my right heel, a thick strip of black elastic stretches from my left hip-bone to a wall immediately behind it and an immense pane of glass, with a hole for my head to stick through, rests on my shoulders and inclines downwards until it meets the ground just beyond the far rail. My elbows point to their respective hipbones, whereupon both forearms are tightly bound together with thick cord. A cloud floats in the background above the pin, waiting to be hit by my approach, when it will disperse. I glance at it and then at the ball, which now has a black mark on its right side. I look at this over the rims of my glasses and lay the clubface as close to it as possible. There is a watch pocket in my trousers. I move my right elbow against it, at the same time slightly rotating the left elbow. I do this two or three times.

I am sitting on a shooting stick in a barrel on a railway line, bound from the elbows to the wrists, giving an imitation of a myopic greenhouse with a twitch.

I am now ready to swing. Taking care not to break the glass or my bonds, or to fall off the shooting stick or the railway line or out of the barrel, or to drop the knotted towel which is now under my right armpit, and keeping the plumb as steady as possible, the handshake friendly and the stronger eye continually on the black mark, I brush the sole of my club straight back along the far rail until I squarely hit a second peg that has been teed into the same rail some six to eight inches behind the ball. At the same time I breathe the word 'Oh'. The elastic tightens, winding itself round my left buttock. I continue to move the club along a course parallel to, and just beneath, the plane of the pane of glass – which has grown considerably wider on this side of my body – while maintaining the earlier precautions. The elastic tightens still further. I now breathe the word 'Mary', on the second syllable of which I turn into a waiter carrying a tray of glasses.

I am sitting on a shooting stick in a barrel on a railway line, muttering to myself while trying to serve drinks under exceptionally difficult circumstances.

To start the downswing I turn my hips to the left, causing the elastic to snap back in the same direction with fearsome speed, dragging the attached hipbone with it. Still taking care not to break the glass or my bonds, or to fall off the shooting stick or the railway line or out of the barrel, or to drop the knotted towel, and keeping the plumb as steady as possible, the handshake friendly and the stronger eye continually on the black mark, I pull a bell-rope and instantly become aware of my tremendous stored-up power. The speed of my clubhead is incredible. A belt now supports my trousers, its buckle in line with, though not on the same plane as, the ball. I hurtle onwards into the impact area. I turn into a baseball infielder throwing half-sidearm, half-underhand to first, rather after the fashion of Washbrook's flick from cover. Simultaneously I give a two-

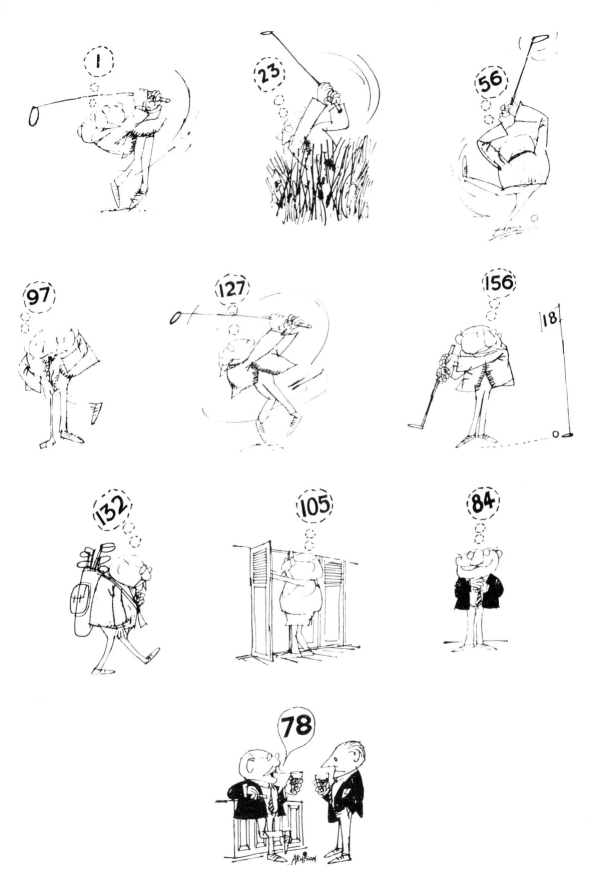

Golf Psychiatrist

An American doctor, who claims a high rate of success in lowering golfers' handicaps by psycho-analysis, is opening a clinic in Britain this summer. DAVID LANGDON drives off first

'I'm at 317 Harley Street – not more than a brassie shot from Baker Street Station.'

*'Couldn't you tackle it the other way round? Iron out my golf swing and **then** have a go at my dementia praecox?'*

'Emergency session. He took ten at the short thirteenth.'

'Could you do us together? She's my partner in the mixed foursomes.'

'Try to hold on. There's a psychiatric unit at the 9th.'

handed basketball pass. At the moment when the clubface finally crashes against the black mark, the string, which originally stretched from the back of my left hand to the pin, reappears on the back of my left wrist and I repeat the first syllable of the word 'Mary'.

I am sitting on a shooting stick in a barrel on a railway line, still muttering, while taking part in a succession of non-golfing activities at a speed which leaves me quite narcissistic with astonishment.

Freed from the glass, the shooting stick, the cord, the string, the towel, the elastic and, in fact, pretty well everything except the barrel, the railway line and the friendly handshake, I now repeat the second syllable of the word 'Mary' and carry onwards at great, but steadily decreasing, speed until compelled to stop.

I am standing in a non-existent barrel on a non-existent railway line, peering in all directions through my existent spectacles trying to see where the damned ball has gone, when all the time it is sitting on the ladies' tee twenty-five yards ahead peering straight back at me.

I am therefore once more standing in a barrel slightly narrower than the last one and . . .

Eric Walmsley
3.4.1963

Dr Golf
Answers Your Problems

Q. *Which is the richest golf tournament in the world?*
A. The Palm Glade Springs $1,000,000 Open Maria Callas/Nat 'King' Cole Open Classic Masters Pro/Am Tournament. It was held only once and the golf course had to be sold for building development to provide the prize money.

Q. *When putting, I have a tendency to hit my left foot.*
A. Have you checked your shoe size recently? It is a common fault among bad putters to wear flashy shoes several sizes too large. Or perhaps you are unusually short-sighted and mistaking your shoes for the ball. One drastic cure, which sometimes works, is to putt standing on your right foot only.

Q. *I have recently developed a tendency when chipping to become nervous about the shot and I can feel my left hand trembling. When I actually play the shot my right elbow feels very weak and I tend to sag at the knees, and my follow-through is spoilt by the club falling from my hands.*
A. You have Partridge's Disease. See a doctor immediately, or take up a game in which a severe disability does not matter, like English Test cricket.

*'Not **too** slow back, sir.'*

Q. *Please help me. My husband has become obsessed about golf, and we very seldom see him at weekends or in the evenings. When he does return he is always in a murderous temper, sometimes drunk, and in a state of manic depression because he hasn't played well. When I try to reason with him, he shouts: 'How would you like it if you bloody sliced every bloody ball you've hit all day, so shut your mouth, woman, unless you want a bunch of knuckles down it!' What can I possibly do?*
A. Tell him to try a shorter back-swing.

Q. *The rules of golf say that if your ball hits your opponent, it is his fault and he forfeits the hole. Does this mean that if you deliberately turned to face your opponent a few yards away and hit the ball straight at him, you would get the hole?*
A. Yes. But he would be entitled to sue you for assault. There is also the danger of hurting him badly, in which case you should ask the next players to play through.

Q. *As a well watered green is easier to putt on than a dry one, I would like to take a watering can round with me so that I can always sprinkle water on my putting line. Is there any rule against this?*
A. This is entirely against the spirit of the game. Golf is intended to be a fair fight against natural conditions.

Q. *Yes, but is there any rule against it?*
A. No.

Q. *Though happily married, I have fallen in love with an older man. My husband does not yet know – though I think the kids have guessed – and I do not know how to break it to him, as the older man is his best friend and they play golf every Sunday. I don't want to hurt my husband, and I am still not sure in my heart of hearts whether I want to leave him. What should I do?*
A. As you are clearly never going to make up your mind, I suggest you invite them to play a special match play game of 36 holes, winner to take you – to make it more attractive, suggest that they wager an additional 25p on each hole. If you would rather just drop a hint, start caddying for the older man.

Q. *I keep having this recurring nightmare in which I am on the eighteenth green with no clothes on, putting for the British Open, and I suddenly notice Jack Nicklaus in a bunker with my wife and I am about to go over and separate them when suddenly the Queen drives past in a caddy car shouting 'It's rude to putt during the National Anthem!' at which point I find my putter is made of rubber and I take eight shots to get into the hole, and even then the hole disappears with my ball.*
A. We all worry about putting too much

HOW TO IMPROVE YOUR SWING

The basic golf swing is made naturally in one easy, rhythmical, fluid action in which the player has only to think about the correct stance, grip tension, arms, legs, hips, shoulders, plexus lumbosacralis, head position, wrists, feet, ball, eyes, clubface, green fees, elbows, wind, thumbs and any local obstructions such as a hill or badly-swollen knee.

COILED

Try to imagine you are a bell-ringer, but coiled through 90° and with a sheet of plate glass extending from your right cheekbone to the inside of your left heel, forming a polyhedron with the V-angle of both flexed index-fingers where they intersect an imaginary line that gracefully arcs *at a tangent* between your neck and the *cosine* of your instep.

Then just follow through as you would when executing a reverse half-pike Zanussi with double twist at water polo.

FEATHERED OFF

A common fault is to mis-hit the ball at the point of impact. Often this is caused by shanking a fat slice, or topping a drawn hook and can only be cured by attention to detail and a couple of hours of concentrated daily practice over a period of maybe 5-10 years.

Make it a habit during quiet moments of the day to exercise your little finger's inner joint pressure point. A useful tip also is to get into the routine of keeping your head perfectly still for two hours or so each morning.

TOPSIDE OUT

If trouble persists with your short game, try switching your attention to your long game for a while, or *vice versa*. Often it will help to change to a high compression ball, buy a new set of matched persimmon woods, or to take a month off work to get the backswing into a repeatable groove.

Theoretically, the ideal golf swing has been likened to a vertical pendulum turned inside out to the horizontal and with a "wristy" fulcrum slightly tilted towards the plane of maximum leverage, largely determined by your height, "feel" and natural tempo. Perhaps the single most important thing is not to thrust or over accentuate.

TRAIPSING AT ADDRESS

Too many "bunched" or "open and shut" shots are caused by lack of tension where the hosel of the club makes a "thin" contact with grass around the ball's lie. Check with groundsman *before* you start the backswing whether the fairway is predominantly bent fescues, poa anna, or an inflorescent raceme with the lemma disarticulate to the glume. Either way, you should square up your shoulders *with* the grain and never snatch, taking special care in wet conditions over the position of your heels.

After the first few difficult years, your swing should soon start to settle into a smooth, instinctive movement. It may feel a little strange at first, but watch a few videotapes of Jack Nicklaus or Seve Ballesteros and try to do exactly what they do in your own

way.

sometimes. Try a different stance and a new club. It often helps to have a change. Once your putting improves, you'll find that all your neuroses about sex, marriage, the British economy and your character inadequacy seem unimportant.

Q. *I need to change my putting style. Can you suggest any alternative methods?*
A. Some of the great golfers have used very unorthodox systems with success. Bobby Prince held the putter with his hands *and* knees. Bangler used to put the club-head behind the ball, then kick it. Sam Wilson jr always putted lying down. Killick believed in oscillating the club like a grandfather clock pendulum, and gradually lowering the club towards the ball till one swing made contact. Charlie Daniels was once asked to analyse his putting style but couldn't; it turned out that for forty years he had been putting with his eyes closed.

Q. *Is there a cure for golf?*
A. No. The Reichling Institute of California was set up to treat addicts ten years ago but has so far not produced one cure. Since then they have lowered their sights and now claim to have a reasonable success rate in ironing out slices and hooks.

Miles Kington
23.7.1975

CHAPTER EIGHT

Caddies

'Golfers as I 'ave Known'
(By a Caddie)

Golfers I divides in me own mind into three clarses; them as 'its the ball, them as skratches it, and them as neither 'its nor skratches the blooming ball but turns rarnd and wants to 'it or skratch anyone as is small and 'andy. The first clars is very rare, the second is dreadfull plentifull, and the third, thank 'evins, can jeneraly be kep clear of by them as knows the ropes. Sich as meself.

Any himprovement in golfers, as a clars, is doo to the 'uge morril hinfluence of us caddies, 'oom some pretends to look down on. Much can be done, even wif the most 'ardened (and some of them golfers is dreadfull 'ardened), by firmness and hexample. 'Show 'em from the fust as you'll stand no nonsense,' is allus my words when the yunger caddies gathers ararnd me fer hadvice. Me being older than me years, as the sying is, and much looked up to. If, as I often 'ears say, there's less of langwidge and more of golf upon these 'ere links, it's doo in no small part to 'im 'oo pens these lines. 'Oo's 'onnered nime is 'ENERY WILKS.

I seldom demmeans meself to speak to the kulprits, for severil reasons which I shall not go into, but I 'ave other meffods. There's sniffing, fer instance. Much can be done by jerdishous sniffing, which can be chinged to soot all cases. Or there's a short, 'ard, dryish larf, but that ain't allus sife. As a blooming rule, I rellies upon me sniff, me smile and me eye. There's few of them as can meet the last when I chuses to turn it on. Not as I objecs very strongly to a little 'onnest cussing; it's

hinjustice and false haccusashun as I will not stand.

Sich are me meffods to them as needs 'em, but don't think, becos at times I'm cold like and 'ard and stern, that I cannot be jentle wif them as call fer jentleness. No blooming errer! 'ENERY WILKS is the lad to 'oom old gents in need of keerfull nussing should be hintrusted by their wives and keepers. I'm not allooding now to old tigers 'oos stiple food is red pepper in 'uge quantitties, 'oo turn upon yer like blooming manniacks if yer blows yer nose quite inercent, and 'oo report yer before yer know if you're standing on yer 'ead or yer 'eels. No, I'm not allooding to old gentlemen like them! 'ENERY WILKS 'as very little use fer sich unguvverned creetures. In 'is erpinyun they should not be let abrord without a chine. But I am allooding to them 'oos pashuns age 'as tamed, insted of blooming well hincreesed, to jentle 'armless old fellers, 'oo will almost eat out of yer 'and, as the sying is, an sich a one is Mister PERCEVAL GIGGINGTON.

Over sixty 'e is, and allus kind and civvil and respeckfull, but 'e 'as no more haptitood fer golf than a jeerarf. Sometimes I thinks, musing kindly like, as 'ow the old cove 'ud be yunger if 'e took the gime less seerius. But 'ENERY WILKS 'as little to reproche 'imself about; 'e, at least, 'as done what 'e could to 'elp old GIGGS. 'Is wife came down to the Club 'Ouse wif 'im larst Toosday, jest as nice an old lidy as 'e's a gent. She drew me on one side and spoke konfidenshul like, while the old man was fussing and bleeting about 'is clubs. It seems as she'd 'eard of me, and 'eard nuthing but good. Which is only right.

''ENERY,' she ses, 'me 'usband 'as set 'is 'art, as you well know, on going rarnd the course in under an 'undred and thirty strokes. It's beginning to tell on 'is 'ealth, the strine and diserpointment, and I wants it stopped. 'E's going rarnd allone wif you now, as the course is clear, and I wants,' she ses, '*I wants you to see as 'e does it!*' she ses.

Well, nobody, excep one ignerrant, gellous, preggerdiced skoolmaster, 'as ever dared to call 'ENERY WILKS a fool. I took 'er meaning in a moment, and I touched me cap, quiet and konfident like. 'Mike yer mind easy, Mum,' I ses in my korteous way. 'It shall be done, this very day, if 'ENERY WILKS is spared,' I ses.

She nods and smiles and slips a bob into me 'and, and then old GIGGS finishes wurrying abart 'is clubs and we makes a start. The old 'un 'ands 'is card to me to keep, and I speaks to 'im, kind like but firm.

'I'll keep the score, Sir,' I ses. 'Don't yer wurry abart yer strokes at all. What you've got to do is to koncentrite yer mind upon yer gime.

For we're a-goin' to do it today,' I ses. 'E 'ears me wif a little sorrerful smile, and I lived up to them remarks. 'E'd arsk me at the end of an 'ole, that 'e'd fairly bitten along, 'ow many 'e'd taken, but I would never tell 'im. I jest kep 'im upon 'is legs wif kindly, jerdishous praise. Even after that 'ole where 'e'd strook me wif 'is ball from the drive, although standing well be'ind 'im, and been in each bunker twice or more, I give 'im a word of 'ope. It was niblick play and 'ope all rarnd the blooming course. And at the end, when I added up 'is card, strike me pink if 'is score weren't an 'undred and twenty-nine! And I sent 'im 'ome to 'is wife, as pleased as any child. There's some, I dessay, as would 'ave made 'is score an 'undred and nineteen or even less, but 'ENERY WILKS 'as allus known the virtew of modderation.

J. R. Stagg
30.5.1906

GOLFING AMENITIES
(*Overheard on a Course within 100 miles of Edinburgh.*)
Hopeless Duffer (who continually asks his Caddy the same question, with much grumbling at the non-success of his clubs). 'AND WHAT SHALL I TAKE NOW?'   *His Unfortunate Partner (whose match has been lost and game spoilt, at last breaking out).* 'WHAT'LL YE TAK NOO! THE BEST THING YE CAN TAK IS THE FOWER FIFTEEN FOR EDINBURGH!'

Beginner (after repeated failures). 'FUNNY GAME, GOLF.'   *Caddie.* ''TAIN'T MEANT TO BE.'

Chastened Diehard. 'MIGHT I TROUBLE YOU FOR THE NIBLICK, COMRADE?'

Mediocre Performer. 'WHAT CLUB DO I USE NOW?'
Bored Caddy. 'TRY A LUCKY DIP, SIR.'

Golfing Rhymes

YOU AND YOUR CADDIE

In private life you may be choicely good,
   Deserve high praise as uncle or as daddy,
You may, in fact, be everything you should,
   But no man is a hero to his caddie.

You may have pictures, priceless curios,
   A famous fiddle (half of it spells Stradi);
You've taken prizes with a home-grown rose,
   But you are not a hero to your caddie.

You've headed expeditions to the Pole,
 Encountered dervishes near Halfa (Wady);
You've set your teeth and done without the dole,
 But you are not a hero to your caddie.

You've written deathless prose and cunning rhyme,
 Composed a song, a second *Yip-i-addy*;
You deal yourself four aces every time,
 But you are not a hero to your caddie.

And yet it is not difficult to be
 A source of satisfaction to the laddie;
Largesse oblige – in terms of £.*s.d.*
 You may become a hero to your caddie.

Ralph Wotherspoon
21.10.1925

'HI! YOU'VE STUNNED A CADDIE!'
'I HAVE? WELL, WHAT'S THE LOCAL RULE?'

The Golfing Gentleman's Gentleman

Devotees of the works of the late P. G. Wodehouse will know that he demonstrated a remarkable insight on the social *mores* of the English upper class. This insight was exemplified by his skilful use of the now vanishing breed of manservant, namely the English gentleman's gentleman. Wodehouse's examples of this genre were always immaculately attired, glided rather than walked, and addressed their masters and mistresses in sonorous tones. Their names, too, epitomised their calling – Beech, Blizzard, Vosper and, of course, the inimitable Jeeves.

What with inflation, the cost of running a stately home and the levelling off of social distinctions, the age of the manservant is past

Golfer. 'REALLY, THESE LINKS ARE DREADFUL!'
Bored Caddie. 'THIS AIN'T THE LINKS. YOU GOT OFF 'EM LONG AGO.'

but there are certain areas where he can still be found, albeit in a different guise. One particular area where the servant/master relationship still flourishes is on the world's golf courses when golfers take it upon themselves to hire a caddie. It is true that caddies are not always immaculately attired and their speech is not always sonorous but their role as hovering confidant, supplier of information, encouragement and sympathy casts them as a sort of manservant of the links.

The word 'caddie' is the Scots form of the French *cadet*, a term applied to the younger sons of French nobility who went to Edinburgh in the train of Mary, Queen of Scots. While Mary paid the extreme penalty for lifting her head by having it removed, the cadets remained and evolved into men, usually skilled at golf who, for a fee, carried a player's clubs and offered advice.

Over the years, caddies and caddie stories have become part of the folklore of the game and many caddies have become equally as famous as those players for whom they worked. In the late 19th century, the caddie sheds of Scotland were the breeding grounds of many great players who later became professionals and supplemented their income either by caddying or looking after the condition of the course.

The first caddie to gain any real fame was one 'Fiery' Crawford who caddied for Arthur Balfour, who later became Prime Minister. 'Fiery' used to say to his clients, 'With my brains and your golf we ought to go a long way', a remark no doubt calculated to ensure a generous tip at the end of the day. In his later life, 'Fiery' set up a ginger beer stall at the far end of the links at North Berwick which did a thriving business, although his weakness for attending funerals meant that, as he got older, the stall was unmanned for long periods. The position of the caddie-cum-professional was still somewhat low down on the social scale. Gentlemen golfers were warned not to tip their caddies too generously since the money would be dissipated on drink. In 1900 the golf historian, Horace Hutchinson, wrote, 'The professional is a feckless, reckless creature. In the golfing season in Scotland he makes his money all the day and spends it all the night.

Caddie (as famous surgeon misses another short putt). 'LUMMY! FANCY BEIN' OPERATED ON BY *'IM!*'

His sole loves are golf and whisky. If he were but ordinarily thrifty, he could lay by in the autumn sufficient to carry him through the season of his discontent when no golf is played. He can lightly earn seven and sixpence a day by playing two rounds of golf or, if he does not get an engagement, three and six-pence a day by carrying clubs. These are about the fees paid at St Andrews and Musselburgh, Scotland.'

As the lot of the professional changed, however, so did the character of the caddie. Instead of being drawn from the ranks of the professionals, they came from the ranks of those who worked with their hands, or artisans as they are still somewhat patronisingly known. They were the gardeners-cum-handymen, men who pottered about doing odd jobs for people and who would present

themselves at the local golf club at the weekends in search of a bag to carry. The caddies of the 1920s were typical of the British infantry soldier, the original Tommy Atkins. Having been through the hell of the trenches, he emerged as a man who knew from bitter experience the futility of wasting breath on unnecessary words. This made him ideally equipped to work as a caddie since golf is a game where silence is often golden and golfers have claimed to have been put off by the uproar of the butterflies in an adjoining meadow.

The period between the wars was the golden age of the caddie and it was during this time that caddies gained the reputation for being ready wits and deliberate humorists for the remarks they made concerning their masters' imperfections on the course. In truth, their

'MY WORD, SIR, YOU *ARE* IN FORM TODAY! THIS IS THE BIGGEST DIVOT I'VE EVER 'ANDLED.'

IF PLAYERS DRESSED THE PART ACCORDING TO THEIR ABILITY TO PLAY —

THINGS WOULD LOOK DIFFERENT.

Golfer. 'WHAT CLUBS HAVE I LEFT?'
Thoroughly fed-up Caddie. 'DUNNO, BUT I KNOW ONE YOU OUGHT TO LEAVE.'

Caddie. 'SHALL I REPLACE THE DIVOT, SIR, OR WOULD YOU LIKE IT FOR THE HARVEST FESTIVAL?'

remarks were usually based on an acute eye for human weakness which, when spotted, was revealed with a penetrating home truth. Their employers took these remarks to be examples of the caddies' wit and so the myth was born whereupon every golfer worth his salt felt he had to possess a fund of caddie stories if he were to hold his head up among his cronies in the bar after a round.

Nowadays the caddie is an international character – he can be a small boy, a law student supplementing his grant or, in some cases, he can be a she, particularly on the Continent and in Japan where caddies can be of such distracting beauty that the employer can find his mind wandering to thoughts of other things. An example of this occurred in Switzerland a few years ago when, during a tournament, a professional engaged a particularly attractive lady caddie and, possibly because his mind wasn't on the matter in hand, compiled a disastrous score. Later that afternoon, another player searching for his ball in the long rough, came across the pair of them. What they were doing has no place in a book such as this but their excuse was that they were consoling each other.

Although caddies come in all shapes, sizes, colours, creeds and sexes, one aspect of their calling remains universal. This is the use of the plural pronoun 'we'. Along with the royal and editorial usage, the caddie 'we' should be accepted as correct, for any worthwhile caddie will not use anything else when talking to his master. 'We want to nudge it up to the left, sir' or 'What we want here, sir, is a good straight drive' are typical of the caddie patois. It must be said, however, that in the privacy of the caddie shed the plural pronoun is sometimes discarded as in 'We had two birdies then *he* went and drove out-of-bounds.'

On the course, caddies soon assess their man and know when to flatter, when to cajole and when to keep quiet. They are expert amateur psychologists driven by thoughts of handsome tip. Scottish caddies of the elder generation still judge a man by the quality of his golf rather than his attributes as a human being. An employer who can't hit the ball past his own shadow is treated with dumb insolence while the employer who can play a bit is made to feel that with a little practice he could take on Severiano Ballesteros.

The real caddies are those who follow the professional golf circuits, a wandering gypsy band whose chief aim is to attach themselves to a player who will win the big prizes from which they will receive a sizeable percentage. These touring caddies are just as hardy as their predecessors but the requirements of the modern game mean that they have additional duties to perform. Apart from keeping the clubs spotlessly clean, they have to pace out

Hopeless Golfer. 'WHAT COULDN'T I DO TO A NICE BIG BOTTLE OF BEER?'
Caddie (scornfully). 'HIT IT WITH A CLUB.'

Caddie (to errant Golfer). 'I NEVER REALISED UNTIL TODAY 'OW MUCH OF ENGLAND IS OUT OF CULTIVATION.'

the course so that their professional knows the exact distance he has to cover to the green from a spot on the fairway; they have to know the location of flagstick on the green and they must be ready on the practice ground to field the balls their master will hit. Even at these exalted levels, caddies can be scathing in their judgement of a player, as witness the case of the young professional who, in testing the direction of the wind, picked up a handful of grass and tossed it into the air. 'What club do you think it is, caddie?' he asked, as the grasses were blown directly into the caddie's face. The caddie bent down, tore a lump of turf from the ground, threw it full into the professional's face and answered, 'I don't know.'

Perhaps the most famous or infamous incident involving a touring caddie occurred during the 1970 Open Championship at St Andrews. The American professional Doug Sanders and his caddie were debating a shot to the green and while such conversations are normally private, an indiscreetly placed BBC TV microphone picked up the following dialogue.

Sanders, 'What's the club?'

Caddie, 'Six-iron.'

Sanders, 'A six? Why not a seven?'

Caddie, 'Naw! You don't want to be xxxx-ing well short.'

And so the wonders of modern technology brought the ultimate obscenity direct into millions of homes and although the BBC were acutely embarrassed, nobody seemed to mind.

It was just another good caddie story.

Chris Plumridge
1986

'WHEN DO I USE THE PUTTER?'
'OH, SOME TIME BEFORE IT GETS DARK.'

The Caddie. 'IT TREMBLED *DISTINCTLY* THAT TIME, SIR.'

'Somehow I couldn't discard him completely.'

*'You want to watch that sniffle of yours, son. It could
turn out to be very dangerous.'*

CHAPTER NINE

Champions and Championships

The Golf Spectator's Round

[Considering that, unlike the lookers-on at any other sport, the crowds who follow golf championships usually have a very much more strenuous time than the competitors themselves, Mr Punch suggests that the Press should report the adventures of the spectators with the same wealth of detail that is lavished upon the doings of the different golfing stars.]

There was a blazing sun and very little breeze when Mr and Mrs Podger went out at 11.15. At the first hole Mr Podger ran up to the edge of the green in fine style and secured a perfect place, but Mrs Podger was trapped behind a woman with a large hat and saw nothing.

Going to the second, Mr Podger was at fault. Owing to over-anxiety he pushed his wife into the bunker on the left of the hole, but recovered brilliantly, dragging her out at the first attempt and landing her close to the pin. Both were well placed at the third, having a nice lie on the soft turf, and Mrs Podger got her breath back. However, she lost it again at the fourth, being well behind Mr Podger in a running-up approach, the latter having now settled down to something like his true form.

At the fifth, Mr Podger reached the green in two sprints and a canter and, if he had not tripped over the ropes guarding the hole, would have further increased his lead. There was little to choose between them from the sixth tee. Mr Podger left himself too much to do with his final spurt, whilst Mrs Podger ran over the green and was strongly reprimanded by one of the stewards.

The strain was clearly beginning to tell, and Mrs Podger was nowhere near with her feeble approach to the seventh. Mr Podger landed in a drain, and, having picked himself out, was forced to work hard with his elbows to get in front. At the next hole Mrs Podger missed three putts on the green through discussing the servant question with a friend. Mr Podger was out in sixty-two minutes, and Mrs Podger in sixty-seven.

On the homeward journey Mr Podger showed an inclination to press unduly, and, though he usually got well away from the tee, appeared to have considerable difficulty in remaining on the greens, owing, no doubt, to the keenness of the officials. At this stage Mrs Podger was hardly ever up and missed many chances of improving her position.

Mr Podger got into serious trouble at the thirteenth through standing on a competitor's foot. Mrs Podger, who had now taken to using her seat-stick very frequently, hardly looked like going much further, and at the fifteenth it was plainly all over with her. Mr Podger finished strongly at the nineteenth hole and completed an arduous round by getting down his gin and stone-ginger before the rest of the field had even reached the bar.

Stanley Salvidge
1.6.1921

ENCOURAGEMENT

Professional Golfer (in answer to anxious question). 'WEEL, NO, SIR, AT YOUR TIME O' LIFE, YE CAN NEVER HOPE TO BECOME
A PLAYER
BUT IF YE PRACTISE HARD FOR THREE YEARS, YE MAY BE ABLE TO TELL GOOD PLAY FROM BAD WHEN YE SEE IT!'

Golf Journalism à la Mode

(*From our Prestlake Correspondent*)

. . . . But of all the duels of giants fought out in this tropical heat none came within measurable distance of the astounding match between Andrew Socketer and 'Wolley' Goggins. Whether we regard the revelation of temperamental idiosyncrasies, the dramatic contrasts or the rapid fluctuations of fortune, the contest was unique and unparalleled in the annals of pastime. As was naturally to be expected the entire company of spectators followed Andrew Socketer in the afternoon. Yet with the pride and affection inspired by the veteran of a hundred fights there mingled misgivings whether, at the age of sixty-nine, he would be able to ignore the strain of having played twenty-seven holes in the morning. Moreover he had so little time for refreshment between his rounds that he was only able to snatch a bath-bun and two aspirin tabloids from the buffet, and wash them down with a split ammoniated quinine and barley-water!

The opening of the match was sensational in the extreme. For the first five holes Andrew was a very tired, frightened old man. He sliced his first tee-shot into the tee-box, whence it rebounded among the spectators. A great groan went up from ten thousand throats and

A DISASTER AT ST ANDREWS
THE COMPETITOR WHO GOT LOST

strong women wept like men. . . . There was a visible shrinking in his bulk, as shown in psychoanalytical snap-shots taken by Professor Buzzard, and the disparity between him and his colossal antagonist was painful to witness.

But Mr 'Wolley' Goggins, instead of kicking his opponent when he was down, was in turn infected by the virus of incompetence. After the fourth hole had been halved in thirteen, Mr Goggins, who was evidently suffering from an acute brain-storm, petrified all those within earshot by saying in sharp staccato accents to his caddie on going to the short

Philosopher (eight down to bogey). 'ANYWAY I DON'T SUPPOSE FOR ONE MOMENT THE CUP IS REAL SILVER.'

fifth: 'Here, give me the knoblock.' Dysphasia had set in, and it affected his play for several holes.

Contrariwise Mr Socketer was a new man from this point and played the next seven holes in twenty-two strokes. The end came on the fourteenth green, when he sank a curly putt with incomparable bravura, and the whole assembly roared their congratulations in full-throated chorus. It was a wonderful achievement for a man just three times the age of his antagonist, half his weight and with barely two-thirds of his calf-measurement. The jubilation of the spectators was, however, perhaps a little speckled with a tinge of disappointment at so fine a player as Goggins being put out of the running. Great and heroic figure though he is, he does not yet possess the synthesis of qualities necessary to bullock his way through a British Amateur Championship.

C. L. Graves
1.6.1921

Brighter Golf

It was resolved this year that the final of the Empire championship should be over eighteen and not thirty-six holes, as other arrangements did not allow of more than a week being allotted to it. The two competitors, Mr Sandbox (Careful and Ancient) and Mr Brassey (Slow-on-the-Wold) are known to belong to the advanced school of golfers, a school which realises the truth of the adage that genius consists in taking infinite pains, and it was considered that three holes a day would put a sufficient, if not an excessive, strain upon their powers. Colonel Eyre Shott acted as referee, and accompanied the finalists in a bath-chair drawn by an ex-service man who had been partially disabled in the Ashanti Campaign of 1874.

The start was advertised for ten o'clock, and punctually at that hour Mr Sandbox, to whom had fallen the honour of taking the opening drive, appeared on the first tee, amid loud applause from a crowd numbering several thousand people. It was rumoured that his opponent was still in bed, having left instructions that he was not to be disturbed until Mr Sandbox showed signs of beginning his preliminary waggles.

Mr Sandbox, after a few moments' silent meditation, devoted a quarter-of-an-hour to an inspection through a pair of binoculars of the fairway to the first hole.

AN INTERESTING INCIDENT

He then walked at a moderate pace to the spot where he anticipated that his drive would alight, a distance of some 250 yards from the tee, and proceeded to make a microscopical examination of the vegetation in the vicinity, crawling about on his hands and knees to do so. These activities were witnessed by the spectators with absorbed interest. Meanwhile, in order not to delay matters, the strength and direction of the wind were being accurately tested with an anemometer, which one of his attendants carried. These details having been adjusted a return was made to the first tee, where immense excitement was created by Mr Sandbox asking one of his caddies to bring him the bag containing his fourteen drivers. Campstools and books were hastily put away, for it was felt that things were beginning to move. A message was sent to Mr Brassey's hotel, and there was some talk of awaking the referee, who had fallen into a peaceful doze. At 10.40 it was announced through a megaphone that Mr Sandbox had eliminated all his drivers except three, and would proceed shortly to a final choice. He was now engaged in deciding which of twenty-three different makes of golf-ball would be best suited to the ground and to the weather.

FIXING THE PEG

The important ceremony of fixing in the ground the small white celluloid peg which Mr Sandbox uses as a tee now took place. Three caddies assisted in this operation, one to hold the peg, another to push it in, and a third to measure the correct height in millimetres. At this juncture there was some interruption of the proceedings, for an intimation was received that Mr Sandbox might after all employ a spoon instead of a driver for his initial stroke. It transpired that he was concerned about three rabbit-scrapes and the mark of what appeared to be a horse's hoof at 253 yards from the tee. In view of the risks involved he thought that it might be judicious to limit his drive to 230 yards. Further reflection, however, decided him to adopt the bolder course and to let himself go, as he phrased it. This resolution was received with acclamation and recognised as being characteristic of the dashing spirit which distinguishes the golf of Mr Sandbox. With the same daring nonchalance he disregarded an announcement conveyed to him by his meteorologist that the wind had shifted the fraction of a point and had stiffened slightly. He merely nodded his head with unruffled serenity.

The peg, which had not been removed, was therefore allowed to remain *in situ*, and after a brief interval a Highflier, Yellow Spot, No. 3, the ball selected by Mr Sandbox for the first hole, was deposited carefully upon it. The spectators, with their nerves strung up to a high pitch of expectation, contemplated for ten minutes the immaculate white globe resting upon its diminutive eminence.

The supreme moment had now arrived, or nearly arrived. The word went round that Mr Sandbox was about to divest himself of his pull-over. The stewards hurried about with ropes, marshalling and controlling the excited onlookers, so as to secure a broad lane for Mr Sandbox's drive.

AN OPTIMISTIC FORECAST

At the apex of the wide angle thus created Mr Sandbox himself was seen lying prone and taking a further and final survey of the horizon. His waggles and trial swings would soon begin, and then, as a cheerful bystander assured us, we should not have long to wait. 'This,' he added, with reference to the preparations we had been privileged to witness, 'is quick work. It is on the green when they are studying the lines of their putts that they like to take their time about it.'

It was the more disappointing that at this ecstatic moment your correspondent became aware that the last train for the South was on the point of departure. As he had the whole forenoon at his disposal he had hoped to be able to describe for the benefit of your readers at least a hole or two, but he is now constrained regretfully to admit that his report is more in the nature of an introduction to the great struggle than an actual account of it. He is consoled, however, by being able to conclude with an important item of information. For on examining an evening paper purchased at Peterborough he learned from the 'Stop Press' that Mr Sandbox had made a good drive, though unluckily a slight hook had carried his ball into the short rough. In a brief interview Mr Sandbox ascribes this misfortune, for it cannot be termed otherwise, to his use of Number 7 instead of Number 10 driver, as well as his neglect to take into account the increased strength of the wind. He will, he adds, devote more attention to his second shot, which he hopes to play some time during the afternoon.

Alfred Cochrane
6.6.1928

A Round with the Pro

If any perfection
    Exists on this earth
Immune from correction,
    Unmeet for our mirth,

The despair of the scoffer,
    The doom of the wit,
A professional golfer,
    I fancy, is it.

No faults and no vices
    Are found in this man,
He pulls not nor slices,
    It don't seem he can;

Like an angel from heaven,
    With grief, not with blame,
He points out the seven
    Worst faults in your game.

'You should hold your club *this* way,'
    He tells you, 'not *that*.'
You hold your club his way –
    It hurts you, my hat!

Your hocks and your haunches,
　Your hands and your hips
He assembles and launches
　On unforeseen trips.

He says you should do it
　Like *so* and like *so*;
Your legs become suet,
　Your limbs are as dough.

He tells you to notice
　The way his club wags;
(But how *lovely* his coat is,
　How *large* are his bags!)

You mark his beginning,
　You watch how he ends,
You observe the ball spinning,
　How high it ascends!

To you the whole riddle
　Is just what he does
When he gets to the middle
　And makes the brute buzz.

He tells you the divot
　You took with your last
Was all due to the pivot –
　Your comment is 'Blast!'

'In his book he sinks it.'

He tells you your shoulders
  Don't sink as they should;
Your intellect moulders,
  Your brains are like wood.

But *he* pulls his wrists through
  Right under his hands,
His whole body twists through,
  Tremendous he stands.

He stands there and whops them
  Without any fuss;
He scoops not nor tops them
  Because he goes *thus*.

Obsequious batches
  Of dutiful spheres
All day he despatches
  Through Time and the years.

You copy his motions,
  You take it like *this*,
You seize all his notions,
  You strike – and you miss.

You aim with persistence,
  With verve and with flair,
You gaze at the distance –
  The orb is not there.

The hands have been lifted,
  The head remains still,
Your eyes have not shifted –
  No, nor has the pill.

He points out the errors
  He told you before,
To add to your terrors
  He points out two more,

Till, your eyes growing glassy,
  Your face like a mule's,
You let out with your brassie
  Regardless of rules.

And the ball goes careering
  Far into the sky
And is seen disappearing
  Due south, over Rye.

You stand staring wildly
  (It's now at Madrid)
And the pro remarks mildly,
  'You see what you did?

You made every movement
  I've tried to explain;
That shows great improvement,
  Now do it again.'

E. V. Knox
23.10.1929

The Walker Cup

[As it might have been reported by the new POET
LAUREATE, if he had happened to be there and had
wanted to do it. The reader is asked to remember
very clearly that the conversations recorded in the
lines which follow are not so much matters of
historical fact as of poetic insight and imagination.]

An hour before the start they talked together,
A pair of golfers in the mild May weather,
TOLLEY and his companion, WETHERED.

For England they had oftentimes been dead.

TOLLEY was large of frame and bold of rig,
Striding the Downs had made his body big.

Stalwart he was, and what he said he felt;
He gave the tiny ball a fearsome welt.
Wide tees he loved and holes with longest carry,
He let into his brassies like Old Harry;
Yet sometimes he could be the very devil
At holing chipped approach-shots to keep level.
In photographs he had a bulldog pipe,
Filled with tobacco from his baccy-kipe.
He loved the mown grass better than deep clover;
He wore a very beautiful pull-over.
The captain, WETHERED, had equal grit;
He made long parks seem paddocks when he hit;
He had the lordliest kind of follow-through
And hit sweet iron-shots. Such were these two.
But now the course was by the bents and sands
And ready for firm sinews and strong hands.
The sun shone high above the German Ocean
(Or the North Sea), which moved with faint emotion.
There was a light wind from the land, not strong,
'The course,' said WETHERED, 'won't play too long.
The greens are quick. The ball that's meant to drop
Or creep up to the hole is like to pop
Over the tin and run a good way past it.'

'I know it is,' said TOLLEY. '—— and —— it!'
'Too early,' WETHERED replied, 'to swear;

'Wait till we find a bunker.'

                                The warm air
Was full of all the scents and sounds of Spring;
Both SMITH and CAMPBELL were inclined to sing
Some sweet old Scottish air like 'Annie Laurie,'
Which they included in their repertory.
'See,' shouted HOLDERNESS, 'the mounting lark
In the blue zenith up above us. Hark!'
But STOUT and HARTLEY cried, 'The only regal
Bird in the air today must be the eagle.'
The team included also T. A. TORRANCE;
They all looked fit and hearty. None wore sporrans.

Sandwich was packed. Lord Bullmonth came from Garp
In a green limousine with Lady Yarp;
The Misses Smythe were there from Tipton Green,
And Colonel Gooch, a rather poor sixteen,
And Wilson, who achieved the Moltby medal
At Wragge last week, defeating Dr Peddle,
And young Jane Isinglass from Scawby Cole,
Who won the Ladies' Invitation Bowl.
Golfers were there from Scotland and from Wales
And the far West, who told each other tales
How they had pulled or sliced into the burn

And triumphed, being two down at the turn.
A Hottentot was talking to a Jap,
Who held a twenty-seven handicap
At Tokio, and all the vivid blazers
And stockings of the girls attracted gazers.
The world had come to see the Walker Cup,

They hoped and prayed that England would be up.

At the top of his form was BOBBY JONES,
Golf was his blood and golf his bones,
All the American courses there are
He had holed at some time under par;
From Oklahoma to Ohio
He had laid the golfing records low,
And was thought by many to be a snip
This year for the Amateur Championship.
He was a hard one to overwhelm,
And so were WILLING and G. VON ELM,
And VOIGT and MOE and R. MACKENZIE
Had driven opponents into frenzy.
Men looked at JOHNSTON, men looked at OUIMET,
'Golly!' they said, 'a darn good team, eh?'
They said, 'It will be a difficult thing
To beat these lads with their lovely swing,
Their lovely swing and their wonderful rhythm
And all the clubs they have brought here with 'em,
Their lovely swing and their beautiful stance
And the way they snatch at the lightest chance,
And the line they take with their ten-yard putts;'
They said, 'These beggars are full of guts;
They hit the ball with the kind of wollop
That a barman deals to a drunken trollop.'

These were the things that men were saying.

Meanwhile the players started playing.
They played two days with a verve and vim
Not to be matched by seraphim.
The crowd was pale. It was dull, elated,
Its heart stood still, its breath was bated.
It ran from the tee to where it reckoned
Was the likeliest place to watch the second;
It stood like cormorants round the green,
The wind came over the sand-hills clean,
The Press photographers moved their shutters
To the sheen of aluminium putters.
A far sail hung in the cloudless offing,
'Gee!' said a guy, 'this is sure some golfing!'
It was drive to drive, it was pitch to run-up.
A woman fainted when VOIGT was one up.
Song cannot sing how steel and wood

Socked indiarubber. Nobody could.
I should dearly like to relate the score
That each man took, whether three or four,
WETHERED working in vain while JONES
Sank his putts as a pond sinks stones,
Hole after hole and round by round –
But man by his destiny is bound;
Fate rings him close, and his might is minished,
I am forced to get my narrative finished
In time to send it along to the paper.

Night fell, and the sea was thick with vapour.

But under the mist the stars came up.

America held the Walker Cup.

E. V. Knox
21.5.1930

Golf Gallerymen Misjudged

I have been a good and painstaking crowds-man at many golf championships and tournaments in the past; but it is only now that I have resumed my shooting stick and striped umbrella for the season proper that I realise how much maligned and misjudged I and my colleagues have been by the sensational press and writers on the game. But never by that gallant gentleman and sportsman, the player himself.

The top-class professional does not abhor companionable, even adoring, jostling round him as he addresses the ball; he knows as well as any film star that when the jostling stops he is on the slippery slopes. 'As long as they leave me my pants,' said a famous American master in this connection . . . But did the statement gain any publicity?

What he does mind, though, is his own human proneness to fallibility – the shaking knee, the suddenly uncocked wrist, the unpredictability of his digestion – everything, in fact, that will interrupt his rhythm and glaze his eye. But the galleryman is blamed if a club is thrown wildly away after a mishit. It is not – or hardly ever – appreciated by the often uneducated writers on the game that because a spectator (who at the moment had been quite reasonably lighting a cigarette from a lighter with a stiff sparking wheel) happens to be hit by the club, the player, nerve-torn, is not indirectly blaming him. No. If the press took the trouble to inquire it would find that the cause of the topped drive was that his hips had let the driver down at the point of impact.

Thomson has never objected to galleryites wearing glasses who turn their heads suddenly into the sun at, say, the tenth; the flash of such lenses was not the cause of the slice; it was Thomson's own delayed reaction to too many slices of cold salmon at lunch. But the press tirade next morning does not spare the poor short-sighted supporter.

A lot of adverse publicity was given to an innocent galleryman on the well-known occasion during the first round of a recent Masters' Tournament. He had managed to push in as far as the eighth row from the front of the ring round the green. While waiting to hear the cheer that would indicate, say, that a five-yarder had been sunk, he began casually to clean out the bowl of his old pipe with a blade of his penknife. It so happened that one of the players chose that moment to lie flat on his back on the green and moan. What were the headlines on the back pages next morning?

'WEETMAN [or Cotton, or anyone else]
MISSES VITAL PUTT
Spectator's Bad Manners at Critical Hole'
No mention, you see, of cramp or spots before
the eyes, or possibly simple exhaustion in the
putter. The faithful follower was blamed.

I have myself seen a former Open champion
– it was, I am nearly sure, during the round
that made him 'former'– laugh heartily at a
woman in scarlet jeans with a pram crossing
the fairway four holes ahead; trying, reasonably enough, to get to the beach (*cf.* Troon any
given championship year). The fact that his
drive had gone into the sea had nothing to do
with this woman. It was due almost entirely to
the unexpected plop of a diving gannet far out
to sea. But the incident started a campaign in
the newspapers against crowds wearing bright
colours during play, although the woman in
question was not even technically a spectator.

Any world golfer, addressing his ball on the
tee of the Railway Hole, St Andrews, takes it
as a personal insult if any given engine driver
does not let off steam when his engine is
passing. Here the engine driver is classified as
a natural spectator, however temporary.
Indeed when the whistle shrills (*cf.*, for
instance, G. Duncan/W. Hagen – Open –
1924) a household name has been known to
stop playing altogether, walk over to the railway line, waving his brassy (or whatever club
comes first to hɩnd) and shout a greeting to the
engine driver . . . Because this interchange
had immediately succeeded a bad case of pull-
ing by Duncan/Hagen, there was a lot of
editorial agitation to have the track taken
up and relaid two miles back from the
fairway. There was no mention, anyhow,
of the player's head having been lifted too
quickly . . .

Fergusson Maclay
10.6.1959

'He lost.'

One Man went to Golf

by GRAHAM

'It bounced back on to the green and he sank the putt for a three.'

'Oh dear . . . !'

'I've read all your books, Jack.'

'Dead straight if you ask me.'

J. W. TAYLOR on

The Open Golf Championship

'Firm grip, head steady, right elbow tucked in – he's a lovely tea-drinker, is that Henry Longhurst.'

Not Just a Game

DAVID LANGDON slices his way into big money golf

'£75,000 prize money
and they waste time looking
for a measly ball.'

'Sorry – consulting your accountant is "seeking advice"
under R. & A. Rule 9(1)(a).'

'I've blown it. How much is second prize?'

'Now take it easy here. All you've got to think of is another ghosted book, the
chance of a new franchise for clubs, shoes, sweaters . . .'

'Don't like the cheering at the 18th – could mean we've put in three days' hard work for a paltry ten thousand bucks.'

'It's up to you, buster. A thousand quid of the prize money if we sink it, or the normal caddie's fee if we don't.'

'Okay, so it's **private** jet lag, flying non-stop from one major tournament to another, but it's still jet lag.'

'Sorry – with the falling pound shouldn't the cheque be made out at the dollar-sterling exchange rate as at the time he sank the winning putt?'

'£5,500 on this putt – talk about the unacceptable face of Capitalism.'

'That Gary Player! All he ever thinks about is sex.'

*'I still dream that one day, please God, I'll get out of the rat race and
put my feet up on an office desk.'*

Says Alliss
*David Taylor talks to **Peter Alliss***

Dear him, straight up, had a marvellous life. What a game golf is. Been some ups, had a few downs, but by and large, he considers, and taking stock of everything, he'd have to say he must not grumble. Keeping cheery is the name of the game. In the moving words of one of Harry's songs, Harry Secombe, and Peter's never forgotten this: *They say I've reached the time of life,/That's slightly past the prime of life,/And yet, and yet, towards the sun I'm turning.* In fact, truth to tell, he's only just turned fifty.

Yet half a century has now passed, so many changes have occurred, since golf professional Percy Alliss, reckoned by some to have been the greatest player never to have won the Open, and Mrs Alliss who played to scratch, were delivered of all 14 lbs of Peter in a bungalow on the edge of Wannsee golf club, Berlin. Marlene Dietrich used to look in, Von Ribbentrop played, yet there comes a time in life when you realise that nothing lasts for ever and Berlin for the Allisses later lost its charm.

So it must be now all of forty years since Peter was a youngster settling into the country of his new home near to Bournemouth, knocking up and down with a set of sawn-off clubs and a ping-pong ball whilst the war went on around him. Pretty soon it'll be 28 years since he came unstuck with his putting at Wentworth and was branded, castigated, reviled, taunted and, all right, pretty shattered as the man who lost the Ryder Cup for Britain.

And then again, let's face it, 23 years, with so many changes taking place all over, have now passed since Peter won three Open championships in successive weeks – the Italian, Spanish and Portuguese. Certainly, certainly, it would have been nice to chalk up the British, if only for his dear old dad who also should have won it, but there you are: the 50s and 60s were turbulent times. Matches were won and matches were lost, there was great materialism, Peter ran to his first Rolls, but there was much sadness and traumatic events besides, including the end of a first marriage and long, anguished days of wondering what was to come.

It does seem extraordinary, looking back, that today there must have grown up an entire generation that knows and admires Peter Alliss only through the modern miracle of TV. There must be youngsters about, some of them taking up the game, who imagine that he's just a commentator and have never read his two fulsome autobiographies.

But then times are very different now, standards are not what they were. Take punctuality, for an instance. If Peter Alliss says he'll see you at 11.30, say, at 11.30 sharp he'll be there. It's not a case of him being there at 11 o'clock or anything of that nature, he stresses, but say by twenty past he'll be in position and all set. It's a virtue that is on the decline, he's observed, and, it needs to be stated, only one example of many such things he could itemise – common courtesy, attitudes to work, attitudes towards the police, this whole business of you mustn't clip kids around the ears. As you get on in life, these things become a little bit depressing, he finds.

For the life of him, Peter Alliss confirms, he's never been able to imagine anything but hard work deserving of success and the rewards which attach thereto. He himself can still recall vividly the first occasion he was privileged to travel by train First Class, or take a trip by aeroplane. Such things had to be earned and were therefore savoured. It is not possible to tell him that more harm hasn't been done by allowing youngsters to suppose that everything is served up for them on a plate than was ever in his day caused by what was imagined to be over-tough discipline.

Mind you, he'll agree, he was something of a renegade once: crusaded for some changes in the game and its whole etiquette. Peter has never found golf remotely difficult. He could play to scratch at the age of 15, could always hit the ball from the time he could stand up, yet was 22 before he got invited into the clubhouse. Even when he was first selected to play in the Ryder Cup, he still felt awkward in the company of some of the establishment. For all he knows, it may have had some slow-fuse effect. Despite formidable talent and a fine record of victories, his tournament career was prematurely kyboshed by a chronic case of 'yips' – nerves up the spout under pressure on the putting green – and he packed in professional play in favour of the box.

At which point in any chat, without fail, the talk turns to Henry Longhurst. No way, Peter wishes to say, does he presume to have taken his place. Not as such. In fact, they got on famously, father-and-son-like. But they were very different, just as the whole feel of the game is today. Money in the main is what's changed it. Huge, unbelievable, obscene amounts of cash are what seem to drive so many players. Of course, Peter says, people tend to imagine he's doing all right from TV and his latest interest in golf-course construction. True enough, not bad, but it's nothing like the big-money tournament circuit. It's funny to think back, but if ever Peter as a young pro was offered £10, it'd never have entered his head to ask for £15. Well, that's all changed right enough.

Peter finds great satisfaction in his programmes combining the pleasures of golf with those of an informal conversation about this, that, and the other. It was especially interesting recently to discover that Jack Jones, whom you might easily suppose is nothing more than a Trades Unionist, is in fact also mad about golf. Interesting, too, is the prospect of a lavish, 7-part TV series on the history of the game, from its earliest stirrings up until the present day. That promises to be something of a microcosm of the condition of man and the way the world has been changing, not always for the better. As you get older, you do tend to find that you philosophise more. Peter would like to have more time just to play golf, but business commitments do so often prevent it. It is an interesting fact that even unto this day, he can still get the doo-dahs over the most straightforward of putts.

This week, of course, he'll be flying to the US Open. It is a great challenge to measure up to the different standards of American coverage of the tournament, they do it rather differently. For the players, too, it'll be a tough Open because Merion is a smallish course, lot of trees, no short cuts, and, on the horses-for-courses principle, that should favour the experienced greats, Watson, Trevino, Nicklaus, and make it tricky for outsiders to spring any surprises. But then, Peter adds, the unexpected is what makes golf so exciting. You don't always get what you think. Or indeed what you deserve.

David Taylor
17.6.1981

Grand Masters

I have never dared ask him to his face, but I am assured in the locker room that this is a true story: some years ago an acquaintance of mine in the west of England was due to get married: he was nutty about golf, a short but straight enough hitter off the tee and only inclined to panic, even club-throwing, when anywhere near sand or scrub. But he stuck at his game. His hero was Jack Nicklaus.

A few days before his Saturday wedding he happened to win first prize in the clubhouse raffle. An air ticket for one to attend the Masters tournament in Augusta, Georgia. The flight was to leave the morning after the ceremony. He said it was too good an opportunity to miss. His bride presumed he was joking – but, sure enough, after a splendid family reception and one night of the cosy connubials he was up early and away for his solo flight. When he returned a week later his wife had flown. He has never set eyes on her since.

Sometimes, when he's putting at the last and into a serene, shepherd's-red sunset over the Bristol Channel, he will pull from his bag a peaked cap bearing the flamboyant badge 'Masters 1972' . . . and every time he arranges it on his head with reverence he offers himself a tiny sigh and gives a momentary rueful shrug before settling over his shoes for the stroke . . . Trouble is, you don't know whether it's his wife, or Georgia, on his mind.

The Masters gets them like that. Though it is a comparative baby – next year it celebrates its half century – the tournament has long been an indisputable biggie in the fixture list of legendary sporting challenges. It has an inner calm, a sumptuous, stylish cool. The TV and radio commentators who will deliver the goods

by satellite this week will all have had to submit to a stern lecture forbidding mention of any other golf tournament ever played except the American and British Opens and their respective Amateur championships.

Nor is money to be mentioned while the play continues – though a very handsome, gift-wrapped bundle of boodle will find itself in the winner's locker. No hint of advertising either inside or outside the grounds: one year a supporter of Arnold Palmer assailed the scene by hiring an aeroplane to fly noisily over the course all day trailing the banner GO ARNIE GO! The organisers wanted to shoot it down.

The Masters was founded by Bobby Jones who, legend demands, will remain probably the finest player the game has known. He retired at 28 in 1930 after playing in only 27 major professional tournaments – as an amateur. He won 13 of them, and at the same time he gained university degrees in law, engineering and English Lit. He looked like Douglas Fairbanks, had the most chivalrous

'Age-wise, he's only one over par.'

of gentle manners, and for the remainder of his life he fought with valour and from a wheelchair a crippling neural disease. Very much in his honour will his tournament be played again this week.

In 1930 a high-powered New York financier, Clifford Roberts, took the shining young renaissance man-child champion to Georgia to see some real estate, an old indigo plantation which had been cultivated for a century – and with gloriously wild abandon – by a Belgian émigré family of horticulturalists called Berckmans. Roberts and a syndicate bought the property for Jones, and with a Scottish landscape artist, Dr Alistair Mackenzie, he built his 'perfect' golf course. Not that there was much work for the bulldozers. As Jones was to write before his death in 1971:

'I shall never forget my first visit to the property . . . the long lane of magnolias through which we approached was beautiful. The rare trees and shrubs were enchanting. When I walked out on the grass terrace under the big trees behind the house and looked down, the experience was unforgettable . . . indeed, it even looked as though it were already a golf course. . . .'

He and the Scottish doctor agreed on the two crucial precepts: fit the golf to the land, not shape the land for the golf; and make it a memorable round for both hero and hacker alike. As Jones put it: 'Two things were essential. First, there must be a way around for those unwilling to attempt the carry; and, second, there must be a definite reward awaiting the man who makes it. Without the alternative route the situation is unfair. Without the reward it is meaningless.'

Putting it another way, he said when the course was opened in 1932: 'I hope it is perfect, for it is both easy and tough; there isn't a hole out there that can't be birdied if you just think; there isn't one that can't be double-bogeyed if you stop thinking.'

Jones and Roberts presented their masterpiece to the United States Professional Golf Association and asked if they would put the course on the rota for the US Open. They were refused with various fob-offs: they preferred 'ocean' courses, Augusta was at its best, 'azalea-wise', in April and the Open was always a high summer fixture etc, etc. It was probably jealousy as well as a niggle at Roberts buying himself in.

So they started a tournament of their own. The first Augusta Annual Invitational was held on March 22, 1934. Roberts's immediate idea had been to call it 'The Masters', but Jones vetoed it, feeling it would be presumptuous so to call a tournament of their own creation. Jones's modesty was always to curb Roberts's megalomania. Nevertheless, the Press got a sniff of the discussion and by 1938 Jones agreed to the official name. Later he was to worry, and admit, 'yes, the name was born of a touch of immodesty'.

The winner each year is made an honorary Augusta club member and awarded the right to wear the club's pale green blazer. He could – and still can – wear it off the club's premises only during his year as champion and only at social golfing functions. Thereafter it is kept for him permanently in a cedar-lined closet in the champions' locker room, where every champion has permanent privileges till death.

It's all good corny stuff from this distance. But the Masters at Augusta, 49 years on, has won itself such a hold in the legend of an ancient game that you scoff at your peril.

Golf – indeed all sport – retains an eye-lowered reverence, a religious solemnity, when hushed talk gets round to Augusta's green jacket. My friend from the west of England is just one of millions. He will stay up late this Sunday to watch the finale on television. He will be alone at his hearth. I am as certain as I can be that he will contentedly sprawl his feet across his coffee table, sup a beer – and be wearing a battered, highly prized, peaked cap bought in Augusta in the week that he was married.

Frank Keating
6.4.1983

Frank
KEATING

"Nobody wins the Open: the Open wins you."

Open Season

It may have been original, or he may have read it somewhere, but Jack Nicklaus hit the very button when he said there were *three* British Opens – 'the one played in Scotland, the one played in England, and the one played at St Andrews'. The asterisk in the calendar of any golfer's decade is winking crazy neon once more this week.

I have attended only one Open at golf's windblown holy of holies – in 1978, when Nicklaus himself won the thing and walked up the 72nd in solo state, garlanded with affection like an emperor home from the wars. Scotland loves him, and the *hurrahs* rose so thick as to make a tangible proscenium over the vast open-air theatre. Afterwards the wise American kissed the battered old urn for the photographers and said: 'I understand the Scots' feeling for me, and they know my feelings for them. Because they understand my feelings

for golf, my feelings for British golf, and for St Andrews and the very history of golf.'

It's not really as corny as the re-telling. Golf, even more than cricket, has long fed off a history of whimsical, chivalrous mystique. No person has so thrived on it as Jack Nicklaus, the game's most stupendous practitioner of recent times. Because Nicklaus understands St Andrews' ancient verity – 'Nobody wins the Open: the Open wins you' – he will again tee off this week as the people's choice as well as the princes' – and far more so than the sombre, suburban Nick Faldo, whatever Fleet Street's jingo might have us believe.

In 1978, Jack played two pretty ordinary opening rounds. He was in the clutch of level-par also-rans. In the third he shot a very decent 69, and before supper that Friday night he went for a short stroll to sniff the air. He sensed a wind was rustling the summer heat-wave evening. He felt the weathercocks might well be pirouetting by dawn. He sat down to eat, silently, his family ignored at the table. Halfway through his baked haddock, he got up and made a phone call. He altered his departure plans from the following, Saturday, night to Sunday morning. More time to celebrate, right? 'The Open wins you.' It had passed on its message.

St Andrews is very special in fiction and in fact. The gaunt, flinty little university town is built around the course. It represents the very definition of linksland golf. Off the North Sea the winds do howl and crack their cheeks – yet within minutes it can be calm again, and serenely still, and the water can be lapping soft at the edges like an inland lake in moonlit, midsummer Italy. And, till this week, I've only been in the place four days!

And, oh, the names . . . the Valley of Sin, the Swilken Burn, Grannie Clark's Wynd, and Bobby Jones's Hole . . .

Jones, the pre-eminent of his day as Nicklaus is in ours, was made a Freeman of St Andrews before his death. In response, he gave moving thanks, not to his new fellow burghers of the town, but to the Old Course itself – 'that wise old lady – whimsically tolerant of my impatience, but ready to reveal the secrets of her complex being, if I would only take the trouble to study and learn.' Jones ended his speech: 'If I could take out of my life everything except my experiences at St Andrews, I would still have had a rich, full life.'

I have enjoyed, for many years, spoiling a good walk with a swipe – but I came late to watching bigtime golf. I suppose it coincided with colour television. Tony Jacklin, in his shrunken little half-mast purple trousers, was the first to wham-bang into my consciousness when he won so chunkily in 1969 at Lytham. Next year was St Andrews – and Nicklaus, in yellow, beat the purple-sweatered Sanders in a play-off, after the challenger had muffed the cinchiest sitter on the 72nd.

I heard years later that poor Sanders, who was a superstitious soul, had, for luck, been given a white tee peg by Lee Trevino, and he had used it at that dramatic last hole. It was the peg which had been used by the late Tony Lema when he had won at St Andrews in 1964. Sanders hit a perfect drive from the tee. Only on picking up the peg did he realise, horrified, that he had gone against his superstition of a lifetime and used a white one. He fluffed his next three, decisive shots.

Lema, who was killed not long afterwards in a plane crash, will, as ever, be remembered warmly this week. Such was his nature, apparently, that some holes before the finish those twenty years ago, he had ordered crates of champagne to be delivered to the Press tent in readiness for celebration.

There have been a number of definitions of how to win the Open. J. H. Taylor reckoned, 'You must effect all your approaches, so you do not need to putt.' For Tommy Armour it was, 'Just walk up to the ball and give it one.' For Jacklin, 'Tempo', for Henry Cotton, 'Controlling at every stroke the tension of the grip in the fingers.' For Tony Lema, the over-riding rule of the Open was, 'No woman-chasing after Wednesday.'

For Henry Longhurst there was a special knack and secret about taking on St Andrews. 'Before playing any shot there, you have to stop and say to yourself, not, "What club is it?" but, "What exactly am I trying to do?"'

There are no fairways in the accepted sense of the word; just a narrow strip of golfing ground which you use both on the way out and the way in, together with huge double greens, each with two flags. So from the tee you can play almost anywhere, but, if you have not thought it out carefully according to the wind and the position of the flag, you may find yourself teed up in the middle just behind a bunker and downwind.

'At that point,' said Longhurst, 'fools say the course is crazy. Others appreciate that the truth lies nearer home.'

Six years ago, the runner-up to Nicklaus was another blond, coiled-shouldered, ex-college boy Yank, Ben Crenshaw. St Andrews had got to him, too. On receipt of his cheque, he was not as effusive as Jack. But just as watery-eyed.

'All I want to thank,' he said, 'is Nature, just for making this golf course.'

Frank Keating
18.7.1984

Opening Time

It is fascinating to watch the practice round on the eve of the Open. It is almost the best day of the Championship. Comparatively few turn up and there is space to watch the great men check and re-check the tool-kit over their caddies' shoulder, to sniff and memorise each zig and zag of the seaside zephyrs, to pore minutely over every hedge and hump and hollow and hillock like so many Brunels squinting into their theodolites. They make copious notes, hit a few hundred golf balls, make more notes, then go early to a restless bed and hope to dream good dreams.

Of course, the largest galleries on practice day follow the visiting giants such as Nicklaus and Watson, Trevino and Ballesteros. Two or three years ago – at either Birkdale or Troon, I cannot remember exactly – I followed the final dress rehearsal progress of young Nick Faldo and his tousle-haired baggage carrier from Ulster, Dave McNeilly. A handful of others were of the same mind as me; Faldo was, after all, Britain's leading player.

In mid-morning, our plodding party of a couple of dozen or so were rail-roaded off our fairway path by a jostling throng four times as big, coming down the other way alongside an adjoining hole. They were frantically and faithfully foot-slogging after a stocky little man on stocky little legs, topped by a stocky little old-fashioned hairstyle. It was Tony Jacklin, the once and former champion who had not won a tournament in years but was still the 'People's Choice'. It was astonishing; you suddenly twigged the word *charisma*. Jacklin was still attracting the home-grown support in spite of Faldo being one of the genuine favourites for the next day's 'world' Championship as well as, on the face of it, seeming a much more appealing fellow, with his square-chinned, open-air, British good looks, his six-footer's frame and meticulously chosen hairdo and natty mix 'n match outfit.

In the couple of years since, I fancy, things have got even worse. The mutual disaffection between Faldo and his own folk can scarcely be lower than it is now. He has not won anything remotely worth a postcard home for over a year and most of the headlines he has made have appeared on the gossip column pages as the spiteful, Grub Street grovellers gleefully continue to root around every remaining titbit of the boy's broken marriage. With each succeeding snide and silly snippet, Faldo has become more sensitive – more surly, if you like. His game has declined in tandem. I hear it said now that he even treats the most admiring, un-enquiring, understanding old plus-foured sports scribbler in the Press Tent as a representative of the mischievous ogres of Fleet Street who are set to do him down. It is a sad state of affairs.

This week the Open comes south again to Sandwich, where sandpipers peck happy on the beach, wild orchids grow in the scrubland, and you can aim some drives at Canterbury Cathedral in the distant haze. Faldo will be, comparatively, playing in his own backyard, for no other course that could possibly host golf's annual jamboree is nearer the young man's home counties' Hertfordshire. I sense a twinge on my bones that he can win the thing outright this week. What price gossip columns then? When Faldo tees off for the first time round on Thursday, it will be his 28th birthday.

He knows well the blissful course, and its sometimes devilish difficulties. It suits him. Sandwich is for concentrators – and few can concentrate with more of a monkish meditation than Faldo. That's another reason the British have never really taken to him; he doesn't wave 'Hi!' as he strolls past. Sandwich is also, somehow, a course to take a man out of himself, to lighten a heavy spirit, to make carefree dull care. It might just be the place to make Master Nick feel snug home again, and allow him to shrug off his frump and his grump.

Walter Hagen, who won there so flamboyantly over half a century ago, was moved to define, 'Don't hurry, don't worry: and be sure to smell the flowers on the way.' One of the best after-dinner speeches I remember was made at the Champions' Supper by William Deedes on the eve of the last Sandwich Open in 1981. The reigning champion, Tom Watson, sat next to him, shaking his head in wonder. It might not have been what he said, but it was certainly the way that he said it. I borrowed a wine waiter's pencil to crib a gem or two on the back of the menu. Next morning, in the cold light of Kent, I could not read a word of my drunken scrawl. Cheats never prosper.

Then, only a few weeks ago (while watching an extremely tedious innings by Surrey at The Oval, as it happens), I picked up the new-fangled, fogey-bright 'country weekly', *The Field*, to discover a piece on the Royal St George's course at Sandwich by the same Mr Deedes. There was a splendid aside about Mr D himself and E. W. Swanton playing a four-some against Ian 'My name is Bond, James Bond' Fleming for what amounted in those days to the *Telegraph* men's combined mortgage – which had probably set the Sandwich Town Hall banquet on a roar that evening in 1981. There was also some Hagen-like appreciation and applause for the very links itself (or is it 'themselves'?), which must be remembered this week when the golfing pundits get going with their course considerations – 'formidable', 'a monster', 'savage rough' and so on.

What could calm Nick Faldo's furrowed brow might be such English strength and civility that the course itself affords. 'Playing St George's', says Deedes, 'is like trying to read the mind of a beautiful woman. It can be difficult but it is never onerous . . . It is for reading, not bashing. You can be in the soup at St George's, but it is delicious.'

Faldo with his 'all court' game seems to me to be suited to St George's as few others in the field. He can open his shoulders and drive furlong upon furlong. With his irons, he has the knack to get *under* the winds so the ball whistles true, shoulder high, like a rifle bullet. On the greens, he has as soft a touch as a camp and well-trained hairdresser.

Also, and crucially, Faldo is a winner. He *has* kept rigidly steady when pressures mount in a final round. His one-time circuit nickname (perhaps sponsored abroad uneasily by some Ballesteros-favouring Latins) *El Foldo* was at once shown to be patently unfair and simply untenable. He remains the only British player to win in the United States since the outstanding Jacklin, 15 years ago, and in the Ryder Cup he has been both bold and unde-feated in any singles matches he has played. Yet his own nation already looks on him, as they do reasonably with British tennis players at Wimbledon, as a no-hoper full only of promise for the first-day's optimistic banner headlines.

Faldo at 28 can be said to be just on the cusp of his prime. If only he himself could understand that. How different, too, in days of old. No hassle then.

The founder of modern golf writing, the Cardus of the Courses, Bernard Darwin of *The Times*, extravagantly left the Press Tent after Max Faulkner had won the Open at Portrush in 1951 – when Faldo was minus-7 – and was persuaded, uniquely, to come in to talk to Fleet Street. Growled Darwin: 'My readers want to read what *I* thought of his performance, not what *he* might have thought of it himself.' (Fifty-one years ago, when Henry Cotton won at Royal St George's, Darwin watched just the first two holes of the Englishman's famous round of 65 – hence the name still of the Dunlop ball he was using – and then signed off his column for the day with, 'Then it was time to go to tea').

Poor Nick Faldo was only 26 when a writer proposed a biography. John Hopkins made a remarkable fist of putting the young man *In Perspective* (Allen & Unwin, £9.95). It cannot, in the circumstances, have been a relaxed or relaxing project. Hopkins had been a popular and admired recorder of the boozy bonhomie of the rugby union circuit for the *Sunday Times*. Pro golf was a different kettle of club; Faldo especially a different kettle of cub. Recalls Hopkins:

'Golf pros played their round, often with little visible pleasure, signed their card and disappeared. Some would return later and head for the practice ground or putting green and Faldo, I noticed, seemed always to be one of the last to leave. I also found out quite soon that he was a loner. I like that. There were not many loners in rugby. Other journalists talked of tantrums and of his not always co-operating with them . . . I was intrigued. Did we have a winner at last? Was Faldo a man who wanted to win more than he wanted to be graceful in coming second?'

I daresay Faldo winced at Hopkins's

portrait. It is by no means a run of the mill, rub of the green, massage parlour job which is usually the way of these things. Gossip columnists would study it if they were *truly* interested in plain facts of a young couple's distressing break-up. The book is short on golf but long on the longueurs of the circuit – and the longing of ambition.

Nick is the only son of George and Joyce Faldo, of Knella Road, Welwyn Garden City. George worked for ICI Plastics and Joyce as a pattern cutter and drafter for Cresta Silks. Dad was hot-stuff at amateur dramatics. Mum was her young man's driving force. She thought and hoped young Nick might be an actor, another Laurence Olivier. 'Then we took him to dancing and elocution lessons. We tried to interest him in music. We knew he'd win the Tchaikovsky piano prize. He had smashing legs and I wanted him to be a model so I used to take him to Harrods' fashion shows. Finally we realised he was only interested in sport.'

He was a stunningly good sportsman with a natural hand-eye co-ordination. But not team games. Already the concentrating, concentrated loner, he might have taken up swimming seriously, or cycling, which he enjoyed. But in the spring of 1971, not long after Mum and Dad had bought a colour television set, Nick stayed up to watch an ITV transmission which featured Jack Nicklaus playing in the Masters at Augusta. He was transfixed. Within a week his school Easter holidays began, and Joyce booked him a lesson at the local golf club. Just before the summer holidays his 14th birthday present for July 18th was a half-set of golf clubs costing £36. The obsession was to be magnificent.

Within four years, on July 26, 1975, quite outrageously, he was English Amateur Champion at Royal Lytham. A year later, on July 10, he shot 69 in the final round of the Open itself at Royal Birkdale, to finish level with Gary Player, Neil Coles and Doug Sanders, at 29th in the whole wide world. He was not yet 19.

Since when, of course, he has been allowed scarcely one soft moment to smell the flowers on the way. Perhaps this week at Sandwich? After all, at Royal St George's, where the sandpipers peck happy, so do wild orchids grow . . .

Frank Keating
17.7.1985

Easy Ryder

I was late in taking a keen interest in big time golf. Sure, I remember Dai Rees's hair-style, and David Thomas's heavy hitting, and Peter Alliss's smarmy Silvikrined locks (and his putting), and Arnie Palmer's steel-thick wrists and carefree, rolling gait. But that was all in monochrome. I was hook, line and sinkered the moment television and young Tony Jacklin's exploits revealed themselves each in glorious Technicolor at the cusp of the Sixties and Seventies.

Jacklin was something special. An authentic working-class hero, the Scunthorpe train-driver's son who swaggered down the middle-class fairways to make sure his chirpy, almost cocky, confidence made him first to slap down his fiver on the bar of the swankiest and most patronising of clubhouses. (Tradition has logged the legend that Henry Cotton had been first to turn a corner for the ordinary working pro golfer in the Thirties, but I can never see that – for Cotton himself was a public schoolboy; he knew the form and was able to turn on the la-di-dah at will.)

In exact tandem with Jacklin's stocky-legged, square-shouldered, little big man's revolution, another fellow was doing the same across the water. Even more so. Lee Trevino had come from a humbler background by far *and* he was taking on the clean-cut, all-American, WASPy blond college boys with a vengeance and a wisecrack.

This week, in the Ryder Cup at the Belfry, near Birmingham, Europe's best dozen play the United States. The two, now middle-aged former ragamuffins who made it, will be doing the ambassadorial hand-shaking and quipping the quotes. Jacklin captains Europe, and Trevino the US. It adds piquancy to what promises to be one of the sporting occasions of the year, as well as an extremely close golf match. Glory be, the home side might even start favourites. Since a St Albans nurseryman and seed merchant, Samuel Ryder, donated a small gold trophy for a biennial team match between the Old World and the New in 1926, the Americans have won the thing an embarrassing, almost shaming, 21 times.

It is bound to be fun with Trevino calling the shots. The man is a one-off, and not only for the sublime way in which he has played his golf. Many barefoot Mexican urchins have grown up to become World Boxing Champions: in the ring, the 'hungry fighter' has been as much a cliché as a reality for centuries. In golf, more than half a century ago, it seemed the Americans might have cracked the code, for the likes of Hogan, Sarazen, Hagen and Snead each came from comparatively humble backgrounds. Palmer, too, I suppose. Since when, two generations of well-to-do college boys have re-established the image. To be sure, not many barefoot Mexicans bother to dream overlong about winning the British Open a couple of times – and then, perhaps, just once more, for luck.

Not, mind you, that Lee Buck Trevino had ever given such things a thought either. Tony Jacklin did, possibly, as he cycled down the Lincolnshire lanes, to and from the golf course after school, or playing hookey from studying for his 11-plus. Trevino did not know his parents. He was brought up by his grandfather in a shack on the tumbledown edge of Dallas. Grandad was an assistant gravedigger. There was little food, less money; bare floors and a barer education. The boy was still a child when he became a scuffler, a conman. There was a golf course near the cemetery, the Glen Lakes Country Club, where, if he was lucky, he sometimes caddied – quickly learning that a Tex White always looks down on a Tex Mex. He scrimped the odd coin, too, at Hardy's nearby golf driving range and pitch'n'putt course. Picking up golf balls.

He taught himself to hit a variety of distances with just one battered old iron club. He started hustling, betting on himself to play trick shots. There were not many dimes in that. There is a sickly American fizzy drink called Dr Pepper. They sell it in litre-bottles. Lee finished one, taped the neck of it for a grip – and played *golf* with it. He drove from the tee, baseball-style, and putted like he was a croquet champion at Hurlingham. The pigeons flocked to take him on. They played with a full set and a caddie. Lee played with his bottle. Incredulous, of course, they wagered good money on themselves. In three years playing with his bottle, Lee never lost a bet.

Such stunts got him a job. By 1965, when he was 25, he was oddjob at the windblown, scrubland course near El Paso, which called itself the Horizon Hills Country Club. He made $30 a week as barman, shoe-shine boy, shower cleaner and ball collector. On the side, he would play members for money. As he won, so stakes got higher. They came from far away to put down the cocky Taco Kid. The hustler continued to win – most times.

In 1967 he returned to Dallas to try for his USPGA card which would allow him to attempt the professional tour. Nobody in the Dallas clubs would even consider endorsing the Mexican's application. He returned to El Paso. The pro there, Bill Eschenbrenner, took a chance. Lee's PGA application form still hangs in his shop, glassed and framed. Eschenbrenner said later: 'He was a pretty tough character then. People were afraid of him. But I trusted him. He vowed he would be loyal to the PGA, and down the line he has proven that a thousandfold. "If you need me, I'll be there tomorrow," he says. I've never known a guy who has got so great but who has changed so little.'

Astonishingly, just one year later, at the Oak Hill Country Club, Rochester, NY, Lee Trevino scattered the field in the 1968 US Open, beating Nicklaus, Palmer and the lot of them by four clear strokes. As he walked down the final fairway, to the stunned last amphitheatre, he slapped a crusty old PGA official on the back and said, 'I'm just trying to build up as big a lead as I can, so's I won't choke at the run-in.'

At that moment was born the image of the crazy, carefree wisecracker. In fact, he is a loner – generous to a fault, sure – but away from the golf course he is a reflective, philosophical man with no need of ebullience in his own company. He may *wear* his heart on his sleeve; but really it remains deep down inside, vulnerable and invisible. There have not been many leading sports figures the public presumes to know so well and yet really understands so slightly. The fine American journalist, Barry McDermott, has studied Trevino over the years. He has a huge regard for him, but explains how it is many moons since young Trevino learned the conman's creed: 'Give people what they expect and want, and they'll believe it and leave you alone. When Lee first played a circuit tournament he'd never seen a gallery or country club blazer, and he didn't know which was the salad fork. He started telling jokes and people laughed . . . With laughter you can do a lot: make friends or a point – or hide a hurt.'

This week, the Trevino of our television screens will be a chirpy, happy-go-lucky Mex, with not much more on his mind than whether the beer is cold. Actually, Trevino is a perspicacious man who can read people the way he can read a green. Will Rogers said he never met a man he did not like. Well, Trevino never met a man he did not know. Yet, by his deeds, you shall know him, and in a way, you log his one-liners, and his throwaways – his lack of boastfulness after victory, his Press Tent generosity in defeat – and over the years, you can build up a fair enough portrait to be going on with. Pat Ward-Thomas, the distinguished British golf writer, was not smitten when he first encountered Trevino. 'I presumed the spate of wisecracks was rehearsed,' he wrote. 'I thought them the work of others, as those of many comedians are. But it was soon clear that Trevino was a spontaneously funny man, also one with a generosity of spirit, not altogether common in a selfish game.'

Nor does Trevino ever forget his background. Here, at random, are a few of his lines I have hoarded over the years. If he will not allow a biographer near, they still serve pretty well as an autobiography:

'There are no rich Mexicans. They make some money – then they call themselves Spanish.'
'My family was so poor, they couldn't afford any kids. The lady next door had me.'

'Grey hair is great. Ask anyone who's bald.'
'When I turn 40, I'm going to go home and count my money. I'm going to have it stacked in bales. I'll just sit there and grin.'
'My doctor told me my jogging could add years to my life. I told him, "Yeah, since I began I already feel ten years older."'
'I plan to win so much this year, my caddie's gonna finish in the top-20 money list.'
'When Chi-Chi Rodriguez and I first hit the tour, our caddie suggested we might use a "sand-wedge". I replied, "Sure, get me a ham-on-rye."'
'The most dangerous thing I do is drive to the bank. I've got a bad stance, a bad swing, and a bad grip. But my bank manager loves me.'
'When Jack Nicklaus came out of his slump I was real pleased for him. "Let him go!" I yelped. "Let the big dog eat."'
'Nobody knows what I'm like at home. My home is private property.'
'They say I'm famous for my delicate chip shots. And, sure, when I hit 'em right they land, just so, like a butterfly with sore feet.'
'My grandaddy said the only way to forget about a woman is go out and find yourself another one.'
'I thought Sammy Davis Junior wore the craziest set of beads – till I was introduced to your Lord Mayor of London.'
'I tell the guys I haven't picked up a stick in weeks; but that's a bunch of bull. I'm no good unless I hit over 300 balls a day.'
'Nobody knows me really. I don't want anybody to know me really.'
'When I won that first "major" in 1968, I enquired about buying the Alamo – to give it back to Mexico.'
'I'm making money, so when I retire in 1985, I hope I'll be set up. If not, well, I'll go pick up golf balls somewhere.'

It is good to have him back – the Captain of America.

Frank Keating
11.9.1985

CHAPTER TEN

Indoor Golf

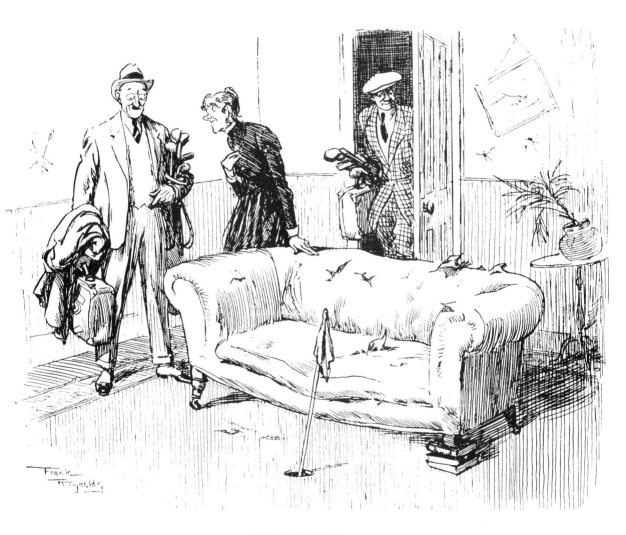

HOLIDAY GOLF

Landlady (*showing apartments in the vicinity of famous links*). 'OH, YOU'LL BE QUITE COMFORTABLE HERE, SIR; YOU SEE, WE'RE USED TO GOLFERS.'

'NO WONDER THAT CHAP COBALT SMYTHE CAN BEAT ME AT GOLF. LOOK AT THE SIZE OF MY STUDIO –

AND THEN LOOK AT THE SIZE OF HIS!'

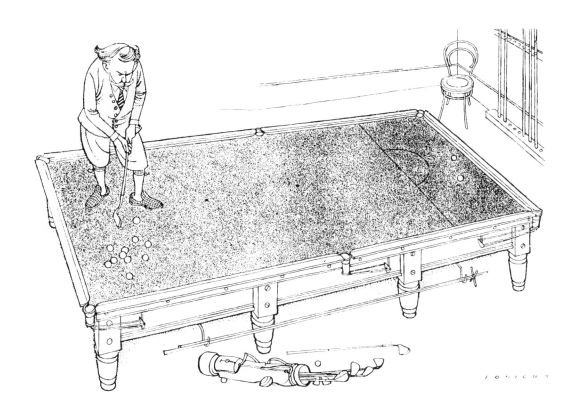

*'What d'you mean –
it is real turf!'*

'How many golf balls have **you** found, Ethel?'

'You're too big for your boots, Fenton.'

'J.T. – don't you think that my standing in this outfit
entitles me to a larger office?'

'Please sir, it's my lunch hour.'

'I have a horrible feeling this is the opening round of a Take-Over.'

Nine Holes Challenge

I long for the links. I want to feel the fresh breeze off the fairway and be dazzled by the bright, golden haze on the bunker. I pine for verdant, artificial landscapes dotted with the delicate pastel hues of Pringle sweaters. I ache for the sight of window-pane check trousers stretched to trapezoids over the golfing buttock.

But here I am, nine stone of ruthless golfing machine, going to waste. Not to seed though. I have never been in better golfing shape but by a terrible irony the very thing that has kept me from the game has honed me to golfing perfection. I'm talking about fertility.

You should see my arms. George Bayer – feel my biceps and weep. Three years of pushing prams has perfected them for long driving. Give me mushy ground, an uphill slope and an oncoming wind and I'll give you 590 yards. My swing leaves nothing to be desired – regular dawn practice rocking 14 lb of teething humanity to sleep has given it a relaxed strength many a pro would envy. Short putting would be nothing to me now; compared to getting runny egg into the mouths of three swivelling heads, it would be a mere bagatelle to get a 1.62 ball into an immobile hole.

I could be out there now, in front of the club house, taking the dinky little fur bootees off my clubs, not trying to get them on my children's feet. What chance have I of a game? Which greenkeeper's eyes are going to light up at the sight of me with my drainpipe golf bag slung across a pram loaded with progeny? Will the nearest golf club open a crèche? In a pig's drainpipe golf bag it will.

But I'm not one to sit here snuffling over my woods and irons, letting my salt tears spoil the finish on my two-toned, fringed golf shoes; I have done something about getting a game. I have built my own indoor golf course. Now Jean Giraudoux said that a golf course 'is the epitome of all that is purely transitory in the universe, a space not to dwell in but to get over as quickly as possible'. Well, I've proved old Jean wrong by building a course in that very bit of the universe in which I dwell. At the moment it only runs to nine holes as the Leeds and Permanent Green committee have not seen fit to fund anything larger. Still, it is full of challenge and idiosyncrasy and will serve till I can return to the real thing.

A well-designed course should make full use of existing features and I have gone to considerable lengths to do this. I have also gone to considerable lengths to cause as little disturbance as possible to the local fauna. I can't say that that particular bunch of ingrates have proved at all grateful for my efforts. The club itself has an informal atmosphere and mem-

A Golfer in the House

by GRAHAM

'Oh God! Don't tell me you've dug out your back numbers again!'

'I clinched it with a twenty-footer on the last green.'

'What d'you think? A three iron or a four wood?'

'The elastic broke!'

'I'm worried about you, Eric! Why not pop round to
the surgery and have a word with Doctor Dixon?'

'He's in the hall, hitting chip
shots into my **best school hat**!'

'Put it off? Because of a little shower?'

'I'll bet Mrs Jacklin doesn't go on at Tony like that!'

bers are not expected to wear ties unless they can't find the cords of their dressing-gowns.

The first hole is the least attractive on the course, taking you over a particularly repellent carpet with one or two greasy patches, then out onto a tiled freeway. Casual water is a very real hazard here as the area is patrolled by two-year-old twins. The hole is in the spin-dryer and I usually use a Number 2 soup ladle.

Tee up for the second hole to the right of the spin-dryer and give the ball a good belt to take it out into the hall. It is here that I have my greatest trouble with that perennial golfing problem – chipping. Believe me, I've tried everything – gloss, trade enamel and yacht varnish but nothing works. One bash with a golf ball and the paintwork flakes off. From the chipped, flaky hall the lie cuts across the front room to an armchair green. The hole is the one buttoned depression that is not full of peanuts and biscuit crumbs.

For the third hole drive out through the bunker and into the front garden. As the club is trying to go up a few social rungs it is as well to make sure no one is taking a bath where we used to keep the coal. It's a sharp dog-leg back through the front door and if you're very sharp you'll catch next door's cat as well. At the moment I usually take it in two up the front steps and into a discarded wellington. Once I've improved at addressing the ball I'll take it in one through the letter-box.

You can see the green for the fourth to the west of the wellington. It looks an easy enough short long into the fireplace, but don't be deceived. Sprawling in front of the hearth is a large area of wild, clinging rough that can present quite a problem. I am sure, though, that deep down underneath she is a very nice girl; it can only be a matter of time before my brother makes clear her somewhat ambiguous position in the household. It is a matter of great relief to all committee members that she is not in the club.

The rise is steep to the next green; up a flight of stairs and into the lodger's kitchen. The big problem here is one you'd expect to find only on a high-altitude course, and that is a lack of oxygen. The artful dodger is much given to boiling up condemned fish-heads for the local feral cats. She is not much given to opening windows. The golfer is presented

'How do you like being on the board of directors, Wilkinson?'

'You mightn't believe this, Parsons, but initially I was utterly opposed to an open-plan office system.'

with the problem of trying to sink a putt as quickly as possible while breathing very, very shallowly.

After firmly closing the door on this malodorous scene, it is just a short drive across the landing, through my bedroom, then into the wide open doors of my wardrobe. I always keep the doors ajar so that my collection of Oxfam's finest silks, wools and linens is on permanent display. I like to let the world see my choice collection of second-hand clothes and it also enables me to call this solitary championship The Classic Open. Hole in a 1940s co-respondent shoe just down and left from the First World War officers' issue trench-coat.

I know other courses run along railway lines but few players can have to deal with such unco-operative railway employees as I encounter. Patiently and often I have explained that Thomas the Tank engine and his mates must stay in their sheds while mater takes a putt on the hearth-rug. I have been met with stares that were blank to the point of hostility. I have been reduced to forging a letter from the Fat Controller allowing me right of way. I don't feel too good about such a deception but awkward lies are the very essence of the game.

It is difficult to get much loft for the eighth hole, mainly because it's bung full of old lavatory cisterns, mildewy tents and yellowing magazines. In my view, an enforced rest would do wonders for this part of the course and an enforced bonfire while we're at it.

Downstairs again for the ninth and final test. This one is usually into the wind as no one else round here seems to bother about closing the back door. The green is on the sloping cupboard under the stairs where the gas meters lurk. It's an awkward hole but it has its compensations. The sloping ceiling forces the player into that hunched lopsided pose that makes for good putting. There are also a couple of rather sickening, yet curiously drinkable, bottles of Uncle Ron's Cherry Brandy that the rest of the club seems to have forgotten about. Pull the door shut, find yourself a space amongst the world's largest collection of plastic carrier bags and you'll find it as amenable as many a golf club. And for a golfing mother of three, a good deal more welcoming.

Susan Jeffreys
1986